核心素养导向的
学科教学丛书

罗晓杰
项纸陆
牟金江 ◎编著

高中英语优质课例

新设计，新说课

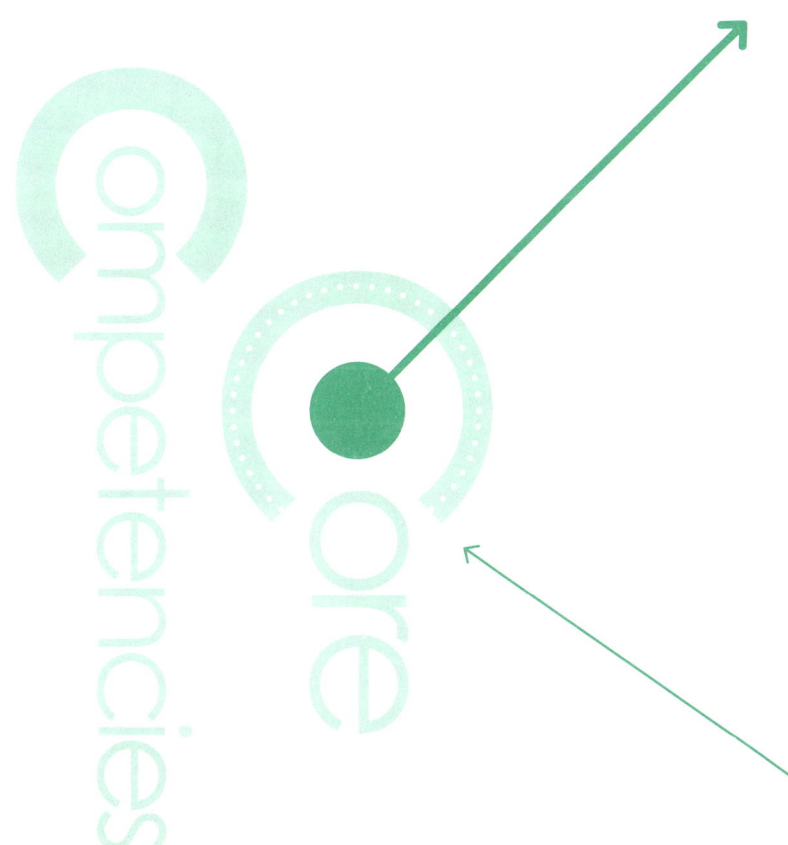

华东师范大学出版社
上海

图书在版编目(CIP)数据

高中英语优质课例：新设计，新说课 / 罗晓杰，项纸陆，牟金江编著. —上海：华东师范大学出版社，2019

ISBN 978-7-5675-8684-0

Ⅰ.①高… Ⅱ.①罗… ②项… ③牟… Ⅲ.①英语课—说课—教案(教育)—高中 Ⅳ.①G633.412

中国版本图书馆CIP数据核字(2019)第046667号

高中英语优质课例：新设计，新说课

编　　著	罗晓杰　项纸陆　牟金江
责任编辑	李恒平
特约审读	陈　琼
责任校对	赵智芳
装帧设计	卢晓红

出版发行	华东师范大学出版社
社　　址	上海市中山北路3663号　邮编 200062
网　　址	www.ecnupress.com.cn
电　　话	021-60821666　行政传真 021-62572105
客服电话	021-62865537　门市(邮购)电话　021-62869887
地　　址	上海市中山北路3663号华东师范大学校内先锋路口
网　　店	http://hdsdcbs.tmall.com/

印 刷 者	上海盛隆印务有限公司
开　　本	787毫米×1092毫米　1/16
印　　张	10
字　　数	216千字
版　　次	2019年11月第1版
印　　次	2023年6月第6次
书　　号	ISBN 978-7-5675-8684-0
定　　价	41.00元

出版人　王　焰

(如发现本版图书有印订质量问题，请寄回本社客服中心调换或电话 021-62865537 联系)

编写委员会名单

（按姓氏拼音顺序）

蔡珍瑞	陈梦梦	陈梦婷	陈学丹	范淑丹
何钰婷	洪晓翠	金灵斌	林颖颖	罗晓杰
牟金江	倪　晗	王惠瑢	王旭碧	夏一建
项纸陆	杨聪聪	余依晨	朱　佳	朱梦佳

前　言

《高中英语优质课例：新设计，新说课》一书主要面向在职高中英语教师、师范院校英语专业学生和学科教学(英语)专业研究生。本书按照评估型说课和教研型说课两类，分别呈现了阅读课、读写课和词汇课等高中英语常见课型的说课实录，以帮助读者更好地把握说课内容、学习说课方法和提高说课艺术。

全书共分为三个组成部分。第一部分：英语学科说课概论。该部分简要介绍了英语学科说课的概念和类型，构建了英语学科说课的内容模块，以"分析"教材和学生、"陈述"目标与方法、"描述"过程与效果、"说明"作业与板书和"反思"亮点与问题等五个模块十个要点为说课的内容框架，进一步介绍了如何说教材和说学生、如何说教学目标和教学方法、如何说教学过程和教学效果、如何说作业设计和板书设计、如何说教学亮点和教学问题等具体的说课方法。第二部分：高中英语评估型说课案例。该部分共呈现七个评估型说课案例(附教学设计)，说课语言为英语。第三部分：高中英语教研型说课案例。该部分共呈现三个教研型说课案例(附教学设计)，说课语言为汉语。

本书的最大贡献是将高中英语说课类型划分为评估型说课和教研型说课，首次构建了"五模块"英语说课内容框架，打破了以往线性说课内容的藩篱，为英语教师科学甄选和优化重组说课内容提供了理论支撑和技术支持，为高中英语教师说课创新提供了更大的空间。本书的另一重大贡献是提供优秀教师的说课视频，在第二部分和第三部分的每个说课案例后附说课视频的二维码，读者可以扫码观看说课视频，对照说课稿和说课视频体会说课的操作方法。多模态的说课示范为规范英语教师的说课行为和提高教师英语说课水平提供了保障。

本书是我国高中英语说课的第一本著作。该书以英语说课理论为基础，以高中英语说课实践为落脚点，既有一定的理论高度，又有很高的实践操作价值，是作者长期从事英语学科说课教学的理论研究与实践探索的智慧结晶。本书的说课案例均由作者与一线教师合作开发,鲜活的说课案例无疑将对一线高中英语教师、英语专业师范生和学科教学(英语)专业研究生的说课实践具有一定的示范与指导作用。阅读本书对高中英语教师和英语专业师范生的教学设计与说课能力的提高有很大裨益。

罗晓杰　浙江师范大学

2019 年 5 月 1 日

目 录

第一部分　英语学科说课概论 / 1

一、英语学科说课的概念 / 1
二、英语学科说课的类型 / 1
三、英语学科说课的内容模块 / 2
四、英语学科说课的内容与方法 / 3

第二部分　高中英语评估型说课案例 / 9

说课案例一（读写课）/ 9
说课案例二（阅读课）/ 21
说课案例三（阅读课）/ 32
说课案例四（阅读课）/ 45
说课案例五（阅读课）/ 58
说课案例六（阅读课）/ 73
说课案例七（读写课）/ 91

第三部分　高中英语教研型说课案例 / 107

说课案例八（阅读课）/ 107
说课案例九（词汇课）/ 122
说课案例十（读写课）/ 137

主要参考文献 / 151

第一部分　英语学科说课概论

一、英语学科说课的概念

所谓说课，是教师在备课的基础上，面对同行或教研人员等，讲述自己的教学设计及其理据，然后与听者互动交流的一种教学研究活动。通常情况下，说课教师要在规定时间内（10—15分钟）把自己将要上的或已上过的某节课的教学设计及其理据用简明、准确、形象、生动的语言（包括体态语）表述出来，有时还要针对同行的疑问进行解释，回答专家的问题，接受同行或专家的评价和建议。

说课要求教师以科学的教育教学理论为指导，将自己对课程标准、教材和学生的理解，对重点、难点和教学目标的把握，对教学方法和学习方式的选择，对教学活动、作业和板书的设计和安排，以及对课堂教学设计与实施的反思进行系统阐述。

说课的总体思路是说明一节课"教什么和教谁——怎么教——为什么这样教"。"教什么"应说清教材、教学章节、课题和具体教学内容，进行教材分析。"教谁"应说清教学对象的知识技能现状和认知特点，分析学生。"怎么教"应在说清教与学的特定内容与方法的基础上，说清为达成教学目标所采取的教学方法、辅助教学的媒体设计、教学活动的设计与安排，通过描述教学过程，包括教学步骤名称、各环节师生主要活动的组织与调控，展示课堂教学的全过程。"为什么这样教"应结合"教什么"和"怎么教"，说清"为什么这么教"的理论依据，包括教学目标和重点难点确定的依据，如学科课程目标和内容标准、单元教学目标、教材内容、学生等，教学过程与教学活动设计的依据，如学科课程标准的教学与评价建议、学科教学理论与方法、教育学和心理学相关理论等。说"为什么这样教"最终要落实到教学过程组织与调控的理据、教学活动设计的意图等方面，落实到教学目标的达成和教学效果的保证。

一言以蔽之，英语说课是指按照说课常规要求，面向同行、教研人员等，使用英语（有时用汉语）分析教材和学生、陈述教学目标、描述教学过程和效果、说明作业和板书设计、反思教学亮点和问题及其原因等的教研活动。

二、英语学科说课的类型

从不同的角度可以将说课划分为不同的类型。最为常见的说课类型划分是按说课目的和用途将说课划分为评估型说课和教研型说课。

（一）评估型说课

评估型说课主要用于评估英语教师的教学与教研能力，通常用于在职教师或英语专业师范生的教师技能竞赛，用于英语教师入职考核、职称评定或教师招聘等。此类说课的语言通常为英语，通过说课评估说课者作为英语教师所具备的专业技能和职业技能，评估说课者的英语学科教育教学能力和教育教学理论水平。

一般情况下，评估型说课本身有时间要求，准备说课的时间也有一定要求，因此，也被称为限时说课，是较为科学的教师综合素质评价手段。对于英语学科评估型说课来说，使用英语说课则更能正确评价说课者的英语教师素质，这是由英语学科的特殊性所决定的。

（二）教研型说课

教研型说课可以进一步划分为集体备课用的教研型说课、课堂观摩前和课堂观摩后的教研型说课。集体备课用的教研型说课一般使用汉语，其操作程序为：指定1—2人先行说课，然后集体研讨，最后综合各方意见，形成最佳的教学设计方案。课堂观摩前后的教研型说课，其主要目的是为评课研讨活动提供上课和听课不能提供或无法获得的备课信息。课堂观摩前的教研型说课其主要操作程序是：说课——上课——评课研讨，参加研讨的教师可以根据教师上课和说课所提供的理论与实践两个方面的信息，把教师课前的"主观"设想（说课呈现）与课上"客观"的教学效果（上课呈现）进行比较、分析和研讨。课堂观摩后的教研型说课的主要操作程序是：上课——说课——评课研讨，参加研讨的教师可以根据教师的课堂教学实况和课后说课反思相关信息展开专题研讨。

一般情况下，教研型说课没有严格的时间要求，被称为非限时说课，是更为规范和更高层次的教研活动。在教研型说课活动中，英语学科使用英语说课还是使用汉语说课没有特殊要求，由于参加教研活动的教师英语水平参差不齐，使用汉语说课更能保证教研效果。目前，我国英语教学界的教研活动通常采用课堂观摩后的教师说课，此类说课目的在于教研，而不是评定英语教师素质，一般采用汉语说课。

三、英语学科说课的内容模块

英语学科说课的内容包括说教材、说学生、说重点和难点、说教材处理、说教学目标、说教学方法、说学习方法、说教学媒体、说设计思路、说教学过程、说教学效果、说作业设计、说板书设计、说教学亮点、说教学问题等。各说课要点之间内容交叉且关系紧密，鉴于大多数说课限定时间，为了避免重复，本书将英语学科说课的内容划分为五个模块。模块一是"分析"，模块二是"陈述"，模块三是"描述"，模块四是"说明"，模块五是"反思"。各模块内容要素相对稳定，模块内部内容可以相互融合，以便灵活应对说课时间和内容要求。具体模块及内容要素如下：

模块一"分析"教材和学生。该模块主要包括说教材和说学生。说教材主要分析教材内容，分析教材的地位和作用；说学生主要分析学生的知识与技能基础、分析学生的学习兴趣和认知风格；分析教材和学生有助于确定重点和难点。

模块二"陈述"目标和方法。该模块具体包括说教学目标和说教学方法。教学目标主要基于教材和学生分析确定，明确重点和难点后基于学情处理教材和选择教学方法。

模块三"描述"过程和效果。该模块主要包括说教学过程（有时只说教学思路）和说教学效果。说教学过程主要按照时间顺序说明本节课的教学活动顺序，描述师生互动过程；说教学效果可以从教学设计的出发点说设计意图，或者从教学实施的落脚点说预设的效果。"描述"过程和效果既要形象生动，又要有理有据，以便帮助听者想象教学过程实施和理解教学活动设计的理据。

模块四"说明"作业与板书。该模块主要包括说作业设计和说板书设计，说明作业设计和板书设计的意图及其对学生英语学习的促进作用。

模块五"反思"亮点与问题。具体包括说教学亮点和说教学问题，有些教研活动也会说再教设计。

对于评估型说课而言，"分析""陈述""描述""说明"和"反思"五个模块都很重要。因为，上述模块内容能够反映出说课者的教学设计与实施能力以及教育教学理论水平。对于教研型说课而言，"陈述"目标和"反思"目标达成情况与教学得失更为重要。因为，听者就在上课现场观摩教学，教学目标、目标达成以及对教学效果的反思更能体现和发挥说课在教学研讨中的作用。

本书没有把教学的重点和难点归到任何一个模块，并非因为它们不是说课的重点。恰恰相反，正是因为它们非常重要，每一个模块都需要关注，需要融合到五个模块之中，贯穿说课的全程。说课教师应结合教材和学生分析，说明重点和难点确定的理据；结合教学目标陈述，明确重点和难点；结合教学过程描述、作业设计和板书设计说明突出重点和突破难点的活动设计和实施方法；结合教学反思说明突出重点和突破难点，达成教学目标的效果。总之，说重点难点是不可或缺的重要说课内容，需要多次与五模块的说课内容融合。

四、英语学科说课的内容与方法

（一）"分析"教材和学生

1. "分析"教材

"分析"教材可划分为宏观和微观两个层面。宏观分析教材主要指对一个单元的教材进行分析。教师要根据单元教学目标和教材内容划分课时，确定课型和重组教材。微观的教材分析是指对某一课时的教材进行分析。教材分析的内容较少，着重分析本课的语言知识与技能要点，分析教材中蕴含的学科核心素养发展要素。

英语说课中的分析教材，首先要简要介绍教材的主要内容、组成部分以及各部分之间的逻辑关系，解读教材的编写意图，分析教材的难易度，介绍本课教材的地位和作用。以常见英语阅读课的说课为例，说课教师首先要介绍阅读文本的题材和主要内容（如果同时说学生，则要简单评价该话题和内容是否为学生所熟悉和感兴趣），然后说明阅读语篇的体裁、文本特征和段落之间的逻辑联系，再分析文本语言的复杂度、语言特色和写作风格，确定学生阅读任务难易度和学生必备的知识和技能，必要时还要分析本课教学内容对本章节学习的影响与意义，说明教材的地位和作用。

2."分析"学生

"分析"学生是对学习者现有语言知识基础和技能水平，思维品质和学习能力等与期望目标之间的差距等要素进行分析。

英语说课中的分析学生是说课的重要内容。因为学习过程是知识不断重组的过程，这一过程必须以学生原有认知结构为基础。因此，教学设计必须考虑学生基础，说课必须要分析学生。

分析学生的内容较多，但基本内容包括以下几点：学生已有的知识经验，包括学生对学习新内容具有的基本的、前提性的知识与技能；学生的学习能力，包括观察判断能力、思维能力、知识迁移能力、知识运用能力、实践操作能力等；学生的年龄特点，包括思维方式、合作意识、注意的广度和持久性；学生的学习态度，包括学习愿望、学习热情、学习兴趣、学习动机等；学生的学习风格，包括思维是否活跃、思维深度和准确性如何，等等。

就英语学科而言，说学生首先要分析学生原有的知识基础和技能水平，要说清楚学生对所学内容是否熟悉，学生现有的知识与技能与本课应达到的知识与技能水平之间的差距，等等。多数情况下，有必要分析学生年龄特点、学习态度、已有的直接经验、学习能力、认知风格，等等。

（二）"陈述"目标与方法

1."陈述"教学目标

"陈述"教学目标是英语说课的重要组成部分。说教学目标通常指说一节课的教学目标，因为说课一般会选择一个课时。教学目标构建主要基于教材和学生分析，主要说明通过本节课教学，学生学得的语言知识、文化知识和掌握的语言技能，以及在学习过程中思维品质、学习能力和文化意识的提升。

教学目标的陈述要结合具体教学内容，将一般性的目标具体化为可观察、可检测的行为目标，要尽量避免使用抽象、笼统的一般描述用语。规范的行为目标的陈述包括行为主体（学生）、行为动词、行为条件和行为表现水平或标准，其中描述行为及其表现水平的措辞十分关键，它决定着教师构建的教学目标体系是否明确、具体、可操作和可检测。

说教学目标必须明确说出语言知识和语言技能等语言能力目标的具体表现，说明在语言能力发展过程中，学生的思维品质、文化意识和学习能力得到了怎样的发展。教学目标可以分条逐一说，也可以分块融合说。分条说教学目标清晰明了，但由于教学目标的各要素间的意义交叉，容易导致语言上的重复性说明。分块说教学目标能够避免冗余信息，但清晰度会受到影响，也容易遗漏。

英语学科核心素养的四维目标是相对可分，相互融合的。因此，说教学目标也没有必要按照四个维度绝对区分,无论逐条或是融合说教学目标,只要能够涵盖本节课的目标要素,都是可以的。因为上述目标均有意义上的交叉,并以共同的教学内容为载体,共同服务于培养学生综合语言运用能力的总体目标。

教学目标陈述也可以结合教学过程、教学反思或教学亮点说。结合教学过程说教学目标,可以说某一教学活动的效果如何,达成了什么目标;结合教学反思说教学目标,可以说本节课教学效果如何,哪些目标达成度高,哪些目标还需要下节课进一步落实。

2. "陈述"教学方法

"陈述"教学方法也是说课不可或缺的部分。从教师教的角度讲,教学方法的选择与使用是决定一节课成败的关键因素。陈述教学方法要说明教师针对本节课的重点难点和学生实际,选择什么教学方法或教学模式,以及如何使用所选的教学方法达成教学目标。

说教学方法要说清以下四个方面:一要说清本节课教师采用的教学方法或教学模式是什么;二要说清在教学过程中教师是如何使用教学方法开展教学活动的;三要说明教师如何运用该方法组织学生参与学习活动,启发学生理解知识和训练技能。换言之,说教学方法要说清在教学过程中教师怎么教和学生怎么学。

说教学方法一般采用集中和分散相结合的方法。集中说是指在教学目标和重点难点陈述之后,简单说明教师在本节课上主要采用何种教学方法或教学模式,并简要陈述理由。分散说是指结合具体教学活动说明教师如何使用该教学方法或教学模式。以英语学科最常见的阅读课型为例,教师要说清本节课将采用或采用了什么教学模式,怎样导入话题,如何组织学生进行读前预测、读中理解和读后产出,如何提问和解答,启发学生进行创造性思维和开展贴近生活实际的交际活动,等等。

(三)"描述"过程与效果

根据说课目的和所给说课时间的不同,"描述"教学过程和教学效果方法也有所不同。教研型课前说课只需简述教学设计思路和教学步骤以及设计意图,而教研型课后说课则无需"描述"教学过程和教学效果,只有评估型说课才要求说课教师"描述"教学过程。

1. "描述"教学过程

"描述"教学过程是评估型说课最重要的内容。只有说清教学过程的具体操作,才能让听者体会到说课者独具匠心的教学设计,才能依此判断其教学理念是否先进、教学步骤安排是否合理、教学活动设计是否科学、教学方法的选择和使用是否恰当、学习方法指导是否到位、重点是否突出、难点是否突破、教学是否有特色有风格、教学能否达成预期目标,等等。

"说教学过程"重在描述,之所以使用"描述"一词,是因为听者需要根据说课教师的描述,想象教学活动如何开展及效果如何。描述教学过程,要按照教学活动设计的先后顺序,依次描述具体教学活动的操作过程,说明教学活动如何开始,如何展开、推进和结束。"描述"教学过程要注意两个要点:一是描述各个教学活动中的师生活动,二是说明教学活动设计的主要意图，必要时还要说明在教学活动过程中生成的问题与对策。具体操作方法如下：

首先，教师简要罗列本节课的教学环节，然后按顺序说明各教学环节所包含的教学活动名称，各活动中师生的教与学行为、活动的设计意图和所需时间。说教学过程重在描述教师的言行，例如，教师下达了什么教学指令，问了什么问题、创设了怎样的情境、学生采用怎样的学习方式学习和操练、说了什么、做了什么、做得怎样，在学生遇到学习困难时，教师如何提供支架、怎样启发诱导、怎样指导学生自主探究、引导学生解决问题，等等。其次，"描述"教学过程中的活动开展情况，还要说明各教学活动的设计意图，即为什么要设计该教学活动，为什么采用该教学手段，为什么选择该教学方法，等等。

2. "描述"教学效果

"描述"教学效果是说课最重要的内容。在评估型英语说课中，说教学效果经常与说教学过程相互融合，即结合说教学过程的各个活动开展情况说明各活动的设计意图或预期效果。事实上，说教学活动的设计意图被视为是从预测教学效果的角度去说，因为预测的效果正是教学活动设计与实施想要取得的效果，二者均可表达"为什么设计该教学活动"。但二者也有细微差异：意图是出发点，效果是落脚点，"描述"教学效果一般指向教学重点突出、教学难点突破及教学目标的达成，即学生在活动中能否学会被列为重点的语言知识和文化知识，能否有效训练目标语言的相关技能，在学习过程中发展了哪方面的学习能力，获得了怎样的情感体验和文化理解等。

"描述"教学效果还有必要从学生学习效果的角度说明学生在学习过程中可能产生的疑惑和遇到的困难，说明教师怎样启发引导，指点迷津，怎样帮助学生排疑解难，走出学习困境。

（四）"说明"作业和板书

1. "说明"作业设计

"说明"作业设计也是评估型说课的重要内容。说作业设计有助于听者了解说课教师检测和巩固学习效果的方式和手段，从而判断说课教师的作业设计能力。虽然该部分在教师说课中占时不多，但缺少对作业设计与布置的说明，会影响教学过程设计的完整呈现，影响听者对教学设计的全面了解。

作业内容、作业要求和设计意图是说作业设计的三个基本要素。因此，通常情况下，英语学科说作业设计至少包括说作业内容、作业要求和检测方法以及该作业的设计意图。说作业布置要求教师说全作业内容、说清作业要求和说明作业设计意图。说全作业内容是说作业设计的首要任务。常规的作业可以简要说明，而非常规作业如角色扮演、小组合作调查等，说课教师则必须详细说明作业的具体内容。说作业设计重在说明作业设计意图。说作业设计意图要说明该作业旨在加深对知识的理解，还是运用所学知识技能；是巩固所学的知识，还是拓宽视野，提升能力。在评估型说课限定时间的情况下，说作业要求，如完成方式和检测标准等常常被说课教师忽视，导致说作业布置信息不全，应该引起说课教师的重视。

2. "说明"板书设计

"说明"板书设计是评估型说课的重要内容。虽然该部分在教师说课中占时不多,但缺少对板书设计的说明,也会影响教学设计的完整呈现。通常情况下,说板书设计要求教师说清板书的主要内容、整体布局及其展开程序,说清板书的设计意图和板书对学生学习的作用。

说板书设计旨在帮助听者了解本课的重点、难点和教学思路。不同类型的说课对说板书设计的要求也不相同。评估型英语说课时,教师可以边说课边板书,板书内容随着说课内容的推进而有序呈现,在说课结束前,板书的主要内容应该基本呈现在黑板上。因此,评估型说课时真正说板书设计用时不多,板书内容与布局只要简单概括即可,重在说明板书设计意图。教研型说课时,由于听者在上课和说课的现场,能够直接感受板书的展开顺序,板书已经在上课后完整呈现,因此,说板书设计也只需说明板书设计意图及其对学生学习的作用即可。

值得注意的是,评估型说课如果给足够的准备时间,说课者可以选择多媒体辅助说板书设计。多媒体辅助英语说课更关注板书内容的完整性和系统性。因此,多媒体辅助说板书设计不宜过于简单,应该逐一说清板书内容、布局特点、展开顺序和板书设计意图,以帮助听者理解教师如何利用板书突出重点和突破难点,领会说课者的教学思路,了解板书设计意图或板书在教学中发挥的作用等。

(五)"反思"亮点与问题

"反思"亮点和问题是说课的重要内容。一般情况下,评估型说课主要反思教学亮点,教研型说课则二者兼顾。

1. "反思"教学亮点

"反思"教学亮点主要反思教学的"得",一般安排在评估型说课的最后环节和教研型说课中说教学问题之前。说教学亮点是对整个教学设计与实施的优点和创新的概括总结。说课类型和说课目的不同,说教学亮点的内容选择也有所不同。

评估型说课中,说教学亮点,可以说教学思路新颖、说教学活动或问题设计循序渐进、说教学方法和教学模式创新、说突出重点和突破难点的方法得当。研讨型说课中,说教学亮点,可以从教师教的角度说教学方法的灵活运用、说教学活动的层层推进、说循循善诱的提问解答等,也可以从学生学习的角度说学生理性的质疑、精彩的回答等创造性思维成果,更可以说师生的默契互动、说教学目标达成等高效的教学组织,等等。

评估型说课中,说教学亮点不必面面俱到,一定要"精"讲,不要"多"说。研讨型说课中,说教学亮点是重要内容。一般来说,教学亮点源于教师对教学的精心设计和师生出色的课堂表现。教学亮点有预设也有生成,多来源于教师有意识的主观努力和师生互动过程中学生的出色表现,是教师独到设计与课堂驾驭能力结合的产物,因此,教学亮点很容易被说课教师自己发现并及时呈现给听者。

说教学亮点切忌泛泛而谈,更不是多多益善。亮点多就等于没有亮点。因此,说课教师应择要而说,并使之条理化,要把教师的教、学生的学和师生的精彩互动有选择性地展示给听者,不但要说清亮点是什么,还要说清为什么是亮点,切忌说空话、套话。

2. "反思"教学问题

"反思"教学问题是教研型说课的重要内容。评估型说课因其备课与说课时间所限,一般不说教学问题。教研型说课因其教研目的和研讨的专题不同,说教学问题的内容选择也有所不同。如果研讨的专题是教学目标落实问题,说教学问题就应该围绕教学目标达成情况,可以说教学重点是否突出、教学难点是否突破、教学媒体选择和使用是否合理、师生互动是否有效、教学活动是否有利于目标达成,而板书设计或教师课堂用语口误等细节问题则不必说。因此,说教学问题并非所有问题都要一一列出,主要围绕本次教研活动的研究专题,反思教学得失,提出需要商榷和值得深入探究的问题。重点围绕影响教学目标达成的突出问题,优先反思与教研主题直接相关的有研究价值的问题。当然,"反思"教学问题也可以简要说说再教设计,具体取决于教师对课堂教学效果的思考深度和对再教设计的成熟度。

第二部分 高中英语评估型说课案例

说课案例一(读写课)

PEP NSEFC M2 U1 Cultural Relics (Reading and writing)

Good morning, everyone. I'm XX from XXXX. I feel more than glad to present my lesson plan here. The lesson I'm going to present is from PEP NSEFC Book 2 Unit 1 Cultural Relics. Now, I'd like to share my plan in the following five aspects, namely, the analysis of teaching material and learners, the statement of the learning objectives, the description of the teaching procedures, the exposition of homework and the blackboard design and the reflection on the plan.

1. Analysis

Now, let's first take a look at the teaching material and the learners. The reading passage is from the workbook on Page 45 titled *Big Feng to the Rescue*. There are altogether three paragraphs talking about the value and possible ways to protect cultural relics. In the first paragraph, we can easily conclude that Feng felt protecting cultural relics important. In the following two paragraphs, we can find Feng's opinion on the value of cultural relics and what he has done to protect the cultural relics. In brief, this is a short passage with a clear structure so it is easy for my students to understand. Besides, the language used in the passage is vivid, for example, *digging down into the earth is like reading page after page of a book*, *old things must be given a place next to new things*. It provides a good example for the students to learn and to appreciate, so hopefully the language will be put into use in their writing. When I was analyzing the teaching material, I came across the Writing Task on page 46. It asks students to persuade a classmate to join them in protecting cultural relics, which can be adopted as a suitable output for the reading passage so that the content and language can be learnt and then used in writing. To sum up, the reading will serve as input, offering the students content and language to write a persuasive letter. The writing task offers a well-structured writing outline. So they are perfectly combined.

II. Statement

Based on the above analysis, I have set the following learning objectives. First, by the end of the class, the students will be able to put the words and expressions they have learnt in this unit into practice, such as *an amazing history*, *a fancy style*, *decoration* and so on. Second, they will apply the language they have learnt in this lesson to their writing, such as *be given a place next to*, *the figure of speech simile*, and so on. Third, they will persuade one classmate to protect a local cultural relic by listing the values of the protection as well as practical ways of doing that. During the learning process, the students hopefully can develop a sense of pride of the culture and civilization of their hometown.

III. Description

Next, let's move to the teaching procedures where I will explain in detail how I will provide opportunities and guidance and offer scaffolds and how my students will learn, appreciate, practice and apply so that all the learning objectives can be carried out.

In this lesson, I have designed six steps. The first step is to activate the schema, which will take 3 minutes. I will ask the students what they have learnt in this unit and what they have known about the Amber Room so that words and expressions learnt will be reviewed. Besides, the schema about the values of cultural relics and the importance of protecting cultural relics can be activated.

After the students are totally warmed up, I will get the students prepared for the writing. The second step is to scaffold for the writing structure. First, I will present a picture of a local cultural relic. The students are going to talk about it and the writing task will be given. Then I will lead my students to have a discussion over how to persuade a classmate named Li Hua to protect this cultural relic. Now, they will still feel it hard to come up with the writing structure and content. So I will ask the students to read the Writing Task part, get some hints and then have a discussion. In this way, they will come up with a writing outline for their persuasive letter. That is, they will do the persuasive writing by analyzing the values of cultural relics and listing practical ways of doing that. This step is not carried out only with the teacher's explanation. The "how" question is firstly solved by the students' previous knowledge, and then by the hints from the textbook and lastly by the ideas from group members. In this step, we can see that learning is not a result but a process where different learning activities are involved.

When the students know how to write the persuasive letter, they still need support in language. So based on the outline done in the previous step, I will ask the students two questions before they read the passage. "Why is it important to protect cultural relics?" "What has he done to protect the cultural relics?" The students will quickly scan the passage, underline relevant information and then share the answers. This task is not hard to do, because, as we have analyzed, the words are easy and the structure is clear. Then with what the students have found, I will ask them to study all the sentences and learn how the words and expressions are used to describe the values of cultural relics and the solutions to protecting them. There are altogether three sentences showing the values of cultural relics, which are worth imitating. For the first sentence, "*old things must be given a place next to new things or people will soon forget their great past*", I will first ask the students what these towers can pass on to the next generation. Possibly, they will give me answers like people's wisdom, ancient art, building technique. Then I will ask them to complete the sentence. New sentences will be made, such as *The two towers must be given a place next to new things so people can pass on wisdom to the next generations*. For the second sentence, "*digging down into the earth is like reading page after page of a book. Each dynasty found in the earth is like an interesting story*", the students will appreciate how simile is used to show the values of cultural relics. Just as what is done in the first paragraph, I will only give the students an uncompleted sentence, like this: ... *is like reading page after page of a book*. And the students possibly can create sentences like *Touching each brick is like reading page after page of a book*. Lastly for the third sentence, the students will practice using the structure "not only ... but also ... ", which is familiar to them. When the values of cultural relics are discussed, now come the solutions to protection. With the hints from the reading, the students will join in a group discussion and come up with more solutions. So answers can be produced like *taking photos to record all these very beautiful cultural relics* and *writing letters to persuade more people to join efforts*. As you can find in this step, the teacher plays an important role in providing tools, guidance and opportunities for students of all levels as I think when the learners encounter study difficulties, it is necessary to provide scaffolds of all kinds.

Now comes the fourth step, which aims to offer scaffold for coherence. I will present an outline only with the first sentence and the last sentence as well as the topic sentences of each paragraph. The students are going to discuss how to organize all the details in a logic and coherent way. Special attention will be paid to the beginning part and the linking words between each part. For example, between the first part, which should be about the background information of the two towers, and the second part, which should include a writing purpose, linking words like "thus" or "therefore" should be chosen and used. All the steps for input will take 23 minutes.

With all the preparations done, the students will feel confident and ready to write their first draft within 8 minutes. I have enough reasons to believe they will write a well-structured letter with proper persuasive reasons in vivid words.

After they've done the first draft, I will collect a sample writing from a student and we will do an evaluation according to a checking list. We will evaluate together in terms of the language used in the writing and the content details which should be well-linked.

IV. Exposition

After the class, the students are going to revise and polish their first draft according to what has been done in the class. This is the homework for this lesson.

Now, let's quickly review what has been written on the blackboard. All the learning objectives can be found here. These are the words and expressions the students will review and learn from the class, which possibly will be mostly used in their letters. The appreciation and use of the language is the focus of the lesson, which will be given enough attention to. What's more, you can also find the outline for reading as well as for writing. Lastly, it can also be found how the students are going to evaluate and improve their first draft.

V. Reflection

Now, at the end of my presentation, I'd like to share my understanding of reading and writing. Actually, practical writing is one of the most frequently used writing activities that occur in our life. So it is wrong to train the students' abilities to do that only when they are in senior three. While they are in senior one and two, the textbook has provided us with lots of well-written passages, which can be adapted for the students to learn and follow so that they can produce nice works on writing. So, this lesson is a trail to integrate reading into writing, where all the activities in the class are designed for the output of the writing. Besides, another shining point lies in all the scaffolds set for the students, making the input agree with the output. Writing is the hardest of all the language skills. So while the students are doing writing tasks, it is a must that teachers design all kinds of activities as scaffolds and support for them.

That's all for my presentation. Thank you for your attention.

(说课稿撰写：温州第二高级中学　项纸陆)

附：教学设计及教材文本

PEP NSEFC M2 U1 Cultural Relics（Reading and writing）

（一）教学分析

1. 教材分析

本课教材选自人教版《普通高中课程标准实验教科书英语必修2》第一单元练习册（workbook）的 Reading Task 部分。该篇阅读主题为文化遗产保护，文本分三个自然段，分别陈述了作家冯骥才对于文化遗产保护的重要性认识、采取的各种保护措施以及他对于文化遗产保护的价值认识。文本内容较简短，语篇话题富含文化价值，文本结构清晰紧凑，不仅是高一学生的阅读佳作，同样适合用于写作训练。文本中多处语言表达生动形象、妙趣横生。如，Digging down into the earth is like reading page after page of a book. 明喻修辞的使用，不仅表达了文化遗产的重要性，也形象地呈现了文化遗产保护过程的探索与传承。因此，笔者整合教材，改编并使用 Writing Task 中的写作任务（劝说一位同学参加当地的文化遗产保护，该任务已经提供了较为明确的写作框架，只要稍加改编即可用于教学），创设情境，使用阅读教材为写作输入语言与内容，使用写作任务为写作提供框架，开设本节读写整合课。另外，作为本单元的最后一节课，使用与阅读单元话题相同的阅读文本，设置旨在运用本单元功能意念项目的写作任务，创设使用单元话题词汇的情境，起到了总结和提升的作用。

2. 学生分析

作为重点学校的高一学生，他们的快速阅读能力和词汇量使得他们能够理解本课阅读文章，能够快速获取信息与语言素材，为当堂写作创造了前提条件。虽然，学生通过一个单元的学习，就文化遗产话题，他们可以调动不少语言，但是这些语言仍免不了"生搬硬套"，缺少生动性。同时，劝说信对于学生而言是陌生的，他们不知使用何种语言劝说，更不知用什么内容劝说。因此，语言与框架的支架搭建是必不可少的。另外，本班学生乐于进行书面和口语的表达，希望能够让听众倾听他们的建议与想法。所以，本课话题与任务必定能够引起学生的足够兴趣。

3. 教学目标

1) 语言能力与学习能力

能够依据单元话题，回顾、提取所学语言知识，产出本单元的语汇；能够理解、欣赏阅读中如明喻等优美表达，并在写作中加以应用；能够通过阅读教材内容、参与小组讨论，获取解决问题的方式方法，从而知道如何写一封劝说信。

2) 文化意识与思维品质

能够通过探讨当地文化遗产，感知前人智慧，产生对本土文化的认可和骄傲等美好情惧;能够通过模仿、创作、修改、评价,在读写活动中,提高低阶思维能力和高阶思维能力。

4. 教学重难点

能够使用丰富的语言和清晰的逻辑结构完成一篇劝说信。

5. 教学思路

本课以文化遗产保护为线索,依据学生的学习能力与需求,从读、写两个角度,为学生搭建四种不同类型的支架,以保证学生高效阅读、高质量写作。支架一,读前搭建框架支架。课堂伊始,呈现写作任务,在任务驱动下,通过讨论、研读教材 Writing task 部分,总结本课的劝说信内容应包括文化遗产的价值和保护文化遗产的措施两个方面。支架二,读中搭建语言支架。在读前活动获得的框架基础之上,学生从价值和措施两个层面阅读文本,获取信息与语汇,理解并欣赏,然后在教师的问题与任务的提示和驱动下,模仿、提炼可用于写作的语言。支架三,写前搭建逻辑支架。呈现写作框架,给出首尾句,要求学生思考段落之间的逻辑关系,并思考使用何种逻辑连接词。支架四,写后搭建评价支架。教师提供评价表,互评例文,提出修改意见,并布置相应作业。

(二)教学过程

1. 教学活动

Step 1:Activate the schema (3 mins)

Review what has been learnt, recall the words and expressions learnt in the previous lessons concerning the topic "cultural relics".

Questions:1. What have we learnt in this unit?

2. What do you know about the Amber Room?

T:What have we learnt in this unit?

Ss:Cultural relics.

T:Any cultural relics do you remember?

Ss:The Amber Room.

T:What do you know about this great cultural relic?

Ss:Amazing, fancy, wonderful ...

S1:It has an amazing history.

S2:It is valuable.

S3:It is in the fancy style.

T:You have learnt so many words concerning cultural relics and now you are using them. Good.

【设计说明】 简单的问题,简单的回顾,起点低,有助于学生快速进入课堂学习状态。重温单元话题词汇,不仅为后面的读、写任务奠定基础,更是激活学生对于"文化遗产"这一话题的相关图式,调动学生已有知识。

Step 2: Scaffold for structure (5 mins)

Talk about two pictures and be informed of what task will be completed in the class. Then discuss in groups to come up with the outline for writing.

Questions: 1. What are the famous local cultural relics?
2. How to persuade Li Hua to protect the cultural relics?

T: Actually in Wenzhou, there are some famous cultural relics. Can you name one?

S4: Wu Ma Street.

S5: Gu Lou.

T: Do you know this cultural relic?

Ss: Jiangxin Island.

T: Yes. The two ancient towers on the Jiangxin Island. What do you know about them? Use the words you have learnt in this unit and give me an account of the two towers?

S6: They have an amazing history.

S7: They have historic values.

T: Good. Are they in good condition now?

Ss: Yes.

T: But they will be in danger over time. So suppose you are going to persuade your classmate Li Hua to join you and protect them. You are going to write him a letter. What will you write in your letter? Open your book and turn to page 46. Read the instructions in the Writing task part, have a discussion and then give me your answer.

Ss: (read, think and discuss)

T: How are you going to persuade Li Hua to join you protecting the towers?

S8: I will tell Li Hua the values of the towers. And I will show him the problems the two towers are faced with. Lastly, I will put forward some ways to protect them.

S9: I want to mention the history concerning the towers.

T: Why do you want to do that?

S9: To show the values.

T: That is a good point. How about you?

S10: I want to describe the details.

T: Why?

S10: To show the values of protecting the towers.

T: So we can conclude that in order to persuade Li Hua, we need to list the values of the towers and possible ways to protect them. I mean the solutions. Now, let's come to the details.

【设计说明】 一般的读写课都是以输入为先,写作任务为后,给学生以"潜移默化"之感。本课,笔者反其道而行之,先布置写作任务,然后逐步提供支架,最后水到渠成。笔者认为,学习也是做事,遇到什么困难,就应该想什么方法。学习就是一个解决问题的过程。因此,先布置任务,让学生知道完成任务的困难所在,后续的读、写活动才能更好地落实在写作中。本环节需要学生讨论,获取任务;研读文本,获取信息;再参与讨论,集思广益。学习的过程性得到很好地体现,也提供了学生一种解决学习问题的资源策略。在任务的驱动下,教师总结提示,搭建阅读、写作支架。

Step 3: Scaffold for language input (20 mins)

Read the passage, find out what Feng Jicai thinks about the values of cultural relics and what he can do to protect cultural relics. Then, study and imitate all the sentences taken from the text, which are concerned with the values of cultural relics and ways to protect them.

Questions: 1. Why is it important to protect the cultural relics?

2. What has he done to protect the cultural relics?

T: Why is it important to protect the cultural relics?

S11: Old things must be given a place next to new things or people will soon forget their great past.

S12: Digging down into the earth is like reading page after page of a book. Each dynasty found in the earth is like an interesting story.

S13: The past is not only for us to enjoy but also for the children of the future.

T: What has he done to protect the cultural relics?

S14: He goes out and does what he can himself.

S15: He persuaded the city government to buy some land in the center of the city so it could not be sold for business.

S16: He and other writers and artists took photos of the old parts of Tianjin.

T: Why do you think he should take photos?

S17: To record.

T: Now, let's back to the writing task. Now, you are going to imitate the sentences and show me how you will persuade Li Hua.

Why is it important to protect the ancient towers?

1. Old things must be given a place next to new things or people will soon forget their great past.

Your try: The ancient towers must be given a place next to new things as they _____ _____.

What can these towers pass on to the next generations?

Reference: people's wisdom/ancient art/building technique (建筑工艺)

Why is it important to protect the ancient towers?

2. Digging down into the earth is like reading page after page of a book. Each dynasty found in the earth is like an interesting story.

Your try: _____ is like reading page after page of a book. _____ is like an interesting story.

Why is it important to protect the ancient towers?

3. The past is not only for us to enjoy but also for the children of the future.

Your try: The ancient towers are not only for us to enjoy but also for_____.

What can we do to protect the ancient towers?

1. He goes out and does what he can himself.
2. He persuaded the city government to buy some land in the center of the city so it could not be sold for business.

3. He and other writers and artists took photos of the old parts of Tianjin.

Your try: 1. We will go out and _____.

2. We may persuade _____ to_____.

3. ...

【设计说明】 对于任何写作行为,语言和内容都是灵魂。本环节在上一环节总结的框架的基础上,学生快速阅读文本,锁定相关内容与语言。因为文本的结构清晰,语言浅显易懂,学生能够快速获得相应语言素材。品读语句,鉴赏词句之美,通过问题和提示,模仿例句,在写作任务的驱动之下,为写作输入语言。同时,作为本课的教学重点,学生的阅读与仿写质量高低直接影响了写作质量。通过语言支架的搭建,不难看出,教师在课堂中的职责是多样的,既是任务的设计者,又是完成任务的引导者。这一过程中,教师还需辅助、评价、提升。每个例句皆以理解为前提,以模仿要点为中介,以创造新句为结果,为写作语言的生动性做铺垫。

Step 4: Scaffold for coherence (3 mins)

Brainstorm what to write and how to link all the details and contents in a logic and coherent way.

An outline:

Dear Li Hua,

Do you know the two towers on Jiangxin Island, which 1. _____? Now they are 2. _____.

3. _____, 4. _____.

They need to be protected for the following reasons. 5. _____. 6. _____, 7. _____.

As far as I am concerned, action should be taken to protect them. 8. _____. 9. _____, 10. _____.

Everyone's effort counts. We are looking forward to your early reply.

Yours,
Li Hua

T: Before you start your writing, I'd like to show you an outline. You can easily find there are several blanks. Now tell me what to fill in?

S18: For blank 1, I will write "have an amazing history".

S19: For blank 2, I will write "in danger".

S19: For blank 3, I will write "Therefore" or "Thus".

S20: For blank 4, I will write my writing purpose.

S21: For blank 5 as well as blank 7, I will show the values of the Amber Room.

S22: For blank 6, I will write "Besides", "What's more", "More importantly" and so on.

S23: For blank 8 as well as 10, I will show possible ways to protect the cultural relics.

S24: For blank 9, I will choose linking words like those in blank 6.

【设计说明】 本环节旨在搭建学生写作前的最后一个支架,即逻辑支架。虽然这个支架对于学优生来说不存在问题,但是对于后进生来说,却是影响其写作效率和写作质量的重要因素之一。因此,教师询问学生如何衔接各个部分,使用何种连接词表达何种逻辑是必要的。

Step 5: First drafting (8 mins)

Write the first draft with a checklist.

Checklist	
1. Are the words and expressions used vivid?	YES/NO
2. Are the reasons for protecting the towers persuasive?	YES/NO
3. Are the ways of protecting the towers practicable?	YES/NO
4. Are all the above language and content well linked?	YES/NO

【设计说明】 写作之前提供评价工具,能够有效地帮助学生监控自己的写作行为,从而有效地落实课堂的读、写目标,学生不至于"信笔由缰",在创造的同时,更是学习、模仿、训练。

Step 6: Evaluating and polishing (6 mins)

Evaluate a sample writing from a student according to the checklist. Polish the first draft under the teacher's guidance.

Checklist	
1. Are the words and expressions used vivid?	YES/NO
2. Are the reasons for protecting the towers persuasive?	YES/NO
3. Are the ways of protecting the towers practicable?	YES/NO
4. Are all the above language and content well linked?	YES/NO

【设计说明】 初稿写作不是一个终点,它是另一个活动的起点。学生的写作往往止于一稿,但是写作能力的提高一定在于修改。在修改的过程中,加深对逻辑的推敲,加深对语言的感

知,加深对内容的提升。另外,修改也是对教学重点的巩固。

2. 板书设计

```
                    Big Feng to the Rescue
persuade
values:    an amazing history, fancy style, decorate;
           be given a place next to new things
           is like reading page after page of a book
           not only... but also
solutions: take photoes--record
           write a letter--persuade
           join efforts--cooperate
```

3. 作业布置

Based on the checklist, polish the first draft.

(三) 教学反思

1. 应用文写作应多联系教材内容

目前,应用文写作作为浙江省英语高考的必考项目,引起了广大教师足够的重视。但是由于应用文的类别多,与教材的结合没有太多前人之鉴。因此,不少一线教师选择高三集中教授,常以背诵范文、套用格式、应试训练等方式训练学生备考能力。此种做法虽然可以短时见效,但是却没有充分利用好该写作形式对学生学习的反拨作用。现行人教版教材以单元大纲编写,每个单元都有相应的功能意念表达,配以相应的阅读文本以及写作任务,其中不少写作任务就是应用文。因此,高一、高二的教师完全可以创新使用教材,以应用文写作为产出,当堂写作,巩固单元话题词汇,使用单元功能意念表达,落实学生语言训练。本课的实践,正是关注了教材设计意图,结合了单元话题、功能语篇等,创设情境,以学生的综合语言运用能力为出发点,从而设计了本课。

2. 应用文写作应多注重支架搭建

写作,作为语言技能中最迟缓发展的技能,是学生最感到恐惧的任务之一。因为在写作过程中,学生会碰到诸多困难。受其思维、语言能力的限制,面对一项写作任务,学生苦于"无从下手",他们难以理清思路,缺少写作逻辑的梳理;他们难以调动语言,缺少必要输入的支持;他们难以衔接内容,缺少逻辑连接词的使用;他们难以修改初稿,缺少自我监控的能力等。因此,在课堂上,教师绝不是给学生一篇范文用以模仿,给一个题目用以练习就可以解决问题的。学生的写作,需要教师搭建各种支架。本课中,笔者依据教材、学生和写作任务,分别搭建了结构、语言、逻辑、评价支架,给学生以写作信心,以保证高质量的产出。

教材文本

BIG FENG TO THE RESCUE

His friends and family call him "Big Feng" because he is very tall and played basketball as a young man. But he is also big in a different way — he fights hard to protect China's past. His real name is Feng Jicai and he has written many novels about life in China. Several years ago, however, he put down his pen for a while and began to protect the cultural relics in Tianjin, where he lives. Once someone asked him why he no longer wrote. He replied that at the moment he felt protecting cultural relics was more important.

Feng loves his hometown. He believes that old things must be given a place next to new things, or people will soon forget their great past. He does not make speeches to get others to help him in his projects. Instead he goes out and does what he can himself. If others follow him, so much the better. One of his biggest projects was to protect the oldest street in Tianjin. Along that street some shops had done business for seven hundred years. Although the city government rebuilt this street, they did save its oldest building. Another project was more successful: he persuaded the city government to buy some land in the centre of the city so it could not be sold for businesses. This area is very important for the history of Tianjin. It was here that the city was first built during the Song Dynasty. Later many treasures were found here.

To Feng, digging down into the earth is like reading page after page of a book. Each dynasty found in the earth is like an interesting story. Not long ago he and other writers and artists took photos of the old parts of Tianjin. The photos were put into a book which was very popular. The money from the book helps his projects. Once, an old man asked Feng to sign the book for him, saying he would give it to his grandson who was not yet born. Feng was glad to do it — he knows that the past is not only for us to enjoy but also for the children of the future.

说课案例二（阅读课）

PEP NSEFC M3 U4 How Life Began on the Earth(Reading)

Hello, everyone! I'm Jenny from Wenzhou High School. I'm glad to present my lesson plan here. The lesson I'm going to present today deals

微课

with the reading passage in Unit 4 Module 3, NSEFC.

I. Analysis

Let's start with the analysis of the learning material and my students' ability which is the basis of the lesson plan. The topic of this unit is Astronomy and the reading passage is, as the title suggests, about the beginning and development of life on the earth. The writer starts with the beginning of the universe in the first paragraph and introduces the formation of the earth in the second paragraph and then explains the importance of water for the appearance of life in the third paragraph. After that comes the most important part of the passage — paragraph 4, which is about how plants and animals came into being one after another. The last paragraph is about the arrival of humans and the negative influence human activities have on the earth. The passage is long and there are some terms of different life forms such as "reptiles", "mammals", "amphibians" which add to the students' difficulty in comprehending the passage. Thus it is necessary to invest two periods to contribute to the students' thorough understanding of the passage.

The lesson plan I present today is for the second period of reading. By the end of the first period, the students have got the main idea of each paragraph and the meaning of new words and expressions. So in this period I will guide the students to explore the structure of the passage and the writers' writing skills which deserve students' attention. For example, to make the passage coherent, the writer uses some discourse markers such as "later", "after that" and "thus". What's more, as the writer considers the whole process as a chain reaction, some words indicating influence, such as "encourage", "allow", are used.

II. Statement

According to the feature of the passage, I will set the first and foremost learning objective of this period. That is, the students can appreciate the passage from the writing perspective and summarize the writing skills. By the end of this period, they will be able to apply the writing skills by offering some persuasive suggestions on solving the problem of global warming and present these suggestions in a logical way.

To help them achieve this learning objective, I've designed five tasks as follows.

III. Description

Task 1 is analyzing the structure of the passage. It will cost 5 minutes. The students will review how the writer develops the topic of the passage by recalling the main idea of each paragraph. Then I will put forward a question — "Why does the writer talk about the universe, the earth and water since the topic of this passage is the beginning of life?" This question helps the students explore the writer's purpose of writing the first three paragraphs. The students will realize it is because the writer intends to show the close relation within these factors that he stresses the necessary condition of the appearance of life.

With this conclusion, the students are ready for the next task — appreciating the writer's writing. This task contains three activities and will cost 15 minutes.

The first activity is to read Para. 3 and find out how the writer shows water is fundamental to the appearance of life. This is a task involving students' critical thinking, as they are required to read the passage from the writing perspective. Some of the students may find it difficult and they may just read the original sentences from the passage. So I will ask students to pick out the details. Of course, I will ask some questions to give them a hint, such as "What is the benefit of citing the scientists' belief?". They will conclude that the writer explains the reason why water is important with details by citing the scientists' belief so as to make the statement justified.

In the second activity, the students focus on the details they find in Para. 3 and pay attention to the writer's diction. The students are asked to circle the verbs the writer uses to show the close relation between water and life. They will find out "allow", "produce", "make ... possible". Then I will ask them to think about the benefit of using these verbs and help them draw the conclusion that these verbs can help to state the relation more clearly and make the passage more logical.

Then follows the third activity. The students should read Para. 4 and judge whether it is developed logically. First, I will ask students to think about why plants appeared before animals. They, of course, will tell me that it is because plants provided oxygen, which made it possible for animals to appear. Then I will ask the students to find out the words which indicate the relation. So they will add more to the list of words indicating influence: e. g. "encourage", "follow". Then, I will ask two more questions. First, "In what order is this paragraph written?" Second, "How does the writer show the order clearly?" These two questions help them discover that the writer uses some discourse markers to show the time order, such as "later", and "after that".

With the skills concluded, the students need a chance to put them into practice before applying them in writing.

That's why I have designed the third task, that is to read Para. 5 and judge whether the writer states the influence of humans on the earth with reasonable details and in a logical way. The students will find out the writer makes the statement acceptable by offering details and quoting what scientists believe and develops the theme logically by using some discourse markers such as "thus", "but", and "as a result of this". This task takes 5 minutes.

Then we will move onto Task 4 — exploring the writer's writing purpose, which will take 5 minutes. The students will discuss with partners why the writer writes about the global warming in the last paragraph. They will come to realize the writer intends to stress the close relation between human activity and the future of life on the earth so as to arouse readers' awareness of protecting the earth.

With this awareness, the students are motivated to give suggestions on solving the problem of global warming. This is the last task of this period, which will last 10 minutes. First, they should brainstorm some suggestions on solving the problem of global warming. The students usually will come up with a solution without any supporting details and thus it is not persuasive enough. For example, they will say "plant more trees". So I will guide them to give details to make it reasonable, for example, the students should tell what kinds of trees are to be planted, where we should plant trees and so on.

After the discussion, they should set down a few reasonable suggestions in a logical way by using the newly-learnt writing skills. For example, if they think of planting trees as an important way, then they should use certain verbs to show the positive influence the solution has. To make it clear, they should use these words (for example "encourage") and writing skills to make the writing logical.

IV. Exposition

At the end of this lesson, I will assign the homework. The students will be asked to improve their suggestions by checking the following points: Do I give a reasonable suggestion? Do I present my suggestions in a logical way? So the homework serves as a task helping them to further apply what they've learnt.

These are my blackboard notes. On the left is the structure of the passage based on which students review and analyze the organization of the passage. On the right are the writing skills summarized in the process, which act as a guidance when students write the suggestions in the last task.

V. Reflection

As you see, in this period I help the students read the passage again from the perspective of writing and finally, the students have the output — giving the reasonable suggestions in a logical way. But the achievement of this objective is impossible without many inputs. Let's go back to see how it is achieved.

The students start with analyzing. Students first analyze the structure of the whole passage and the writer's purpose of writing the first three paragraphs. In this way, they further understand the close relation between the appearance of life and other factors. This understanding is the basis of all the rest activities of this period.

Then they focus on Para. 3 and 4 and appreciate the writer's writing to see how the importance of water is stated clearly. In the process they are guided to summarize the skills on how to develop reasonable ideas in a logical way.

After that, they read Para. 5 and comment on the writing. This activity prepares the students to apply the skill. Lastly, they further apply these skills by writing the suggestions, which is the output of the period. These activities involve the students' critical thinking and contribute to their deeper understanding of the passage as well as their language ability.

That's all for my presentation. Thanks for listening.

（说课稿撰写：浙江省温州中学　蔡珍瑞）

 附：教学设计及教材文本

M3U4 Astronomy

（一）教学分析

1. 教材分析

本课教学内容选自人教版《英语》必修三第四单元 Astronomy 的 Reading 部分 How life began on the earth。这个单元以 Astronomy 为中心话题,内容涉及太阳系、地球上生命起源、宇宙大爆炸、月球探秘、黑洞效应等。主课文是一篇科普说明文,主要讲述了地球上生命的起源。正文共分五段,由宇宙的开端引入,逐段介绍了地球的形成、水的出现对生命诞生的重要性以及生命由低等到高等的进化过程,最后以人类不合理的活动给地球带来的环境问题结尾。课文各段落衔接自然,环环相扣,紧扣"生命起源"这一主题。该文思路清晰、用词严谨,比如作者用了 encourage 和 allow 等词描写生命起源的连锁反应,还用了一些语篇衔接词如 after that 和 later 等表述生命起源的过程。另外,作者引用科学家的观点来充分说明生命起源的条件,使行文有理有据。这些写作技巧是非常值得学生去赏析和模仿的。

2. 学生分析

高一学生对生命起源和物种进化有一定的了解,但由于课文篇幅长,且文中有关物种的

专有名词如 amphibians、reptiles 和 mammals 会给学生的阅读造成一定困难,因此学生对文本用词和写作技巧的赏析需要以对文章基本大意的理解为前提。因此将这节课安排在阅读的第一课时更加合理。在阅读第一课时中,学生通过归纳概括每段的大意,理解了文章主旨;通过画生命起源思维导图理清了生命起源的过程;能够理解与文脉相关的重点词汇,如:fundamental 和 exist 等。但是对于文章中一些表示影响的词,尤其是 encourage 和 allow 这两个词是学生熟悉的词,但是学生熟悉他们表示"鼓励"和"允许"的意思,而文中表示"使……成为可能"的意思比较陌生,因此这节课中需要引导学生关注这些熟词生义。

3. 教学目标

1)语言能力与学习能力

(1)发展阅读能力:通过解读文本各个段落大意之间的关系,推断作者选择文本内容的意图,分析篇章结构,进一步了解生命起源的必要条件,从而达到对文章的深层次理解。

(2)发展写作能力:通过赏析第三段作者对水的重要性的分析,总结出作者的写作技巧,即引用科学家的观点阐述主题,使之言之有理,以及使用语篇衔接词和表示影响的词汇使文本严谨连贯;能写出一到两个较有说服力的缓解温室效应的建议。

2)文化品格与思维品质

通过挖掘作者最后一段的写作意图,体会人类活动对地球环境的影响以及保护环境的重要性,并根据生命起源的必要条件提出保护地球的措施。

4. 教学重难点

本节课的重点是赏析文章语言,总结写作技巧并运用写作技巧写出建议。根据对学情的预估,难点在于从作者写作角度去欣赏作者的用词和语篇衔接,并用自己的语言总结这些写作技巧。

5. 教学思路

这是阅读的第二课时,是一节以读促写的读写课。学生基于对文本大意的理解,去探究作者内容的选择和谋篇意图,然后从语言上去发现作者如何达到这个写作目的。教师先引导学生回顾全文结构,再请学生着重分析第三、四段去感受作者的用词并总结写作技巧。然后学生用前面所总结的技巧去评价第五段,最后在写作中运用,从而巩固写作技巧。总体思路如图:

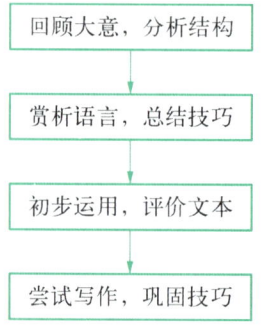

(二) 教学过程

1. 教学活动

Step 1. Analyzing the logical organization

1. Review how the writer develops the topic of the passage by recalling the main idea of each paragraph.

$$\text{How life began on the earth} \begin{cases} \text{Para. 1} & \text{the universe} \\ \text{Para. 2} & \text{the earth} \\ \text{Para. 3} & \text{water} \\ \text{Para. 4} & \text{plants and animals} \\ \text{Para. 5} & \text{humans} \end{cases}$$

T：We have just learnt this passage. What is the main idea of each paragraph?

Ss：...

T：This is the way how the writer develops this topic.

2. Explore the writer's purpose of writing about the universe, the earth and water in the first three paragraphs.

T：The topic is the beginning of life, but why does the writer talk about the universe, the earth and water?

Ss：...（Life is closely related to the universe, the earth and water.）

T：Yes. The writer wants to show the close relation between the appearance of life so as to stress the necessary condition of the appearance of life.

【设计说明】 通过第一课时的学习，学生对文本的大意有了初步的了解。所以在导入环节先帮助学生回顾文章以及各段落的大意，然后引导学生理解和欣赏篇章结构，思考作者在前三段内容选择上的原因和它们对主题展开的作用，促进学生对文本主题的深层次理解。

Step 2. Appreciating the writer's writing skills

1. Read Para. 3 and find out how the writer shows water is fundamental to the appearance of life.

T：Of these three things, which is fundamental to the development of life?

Ss：Water.

T：Why is water fundamental to life?

Ss："What many scientists believe is that .../the continued presence of water ...."

T：So the writer offers a reason to support the importance of water.

T：Do you believe the reason to be true?

Ss：Yes/No.

27

T: How does the writer add to the truth of it? How does he make us believe it is true?

Ss: Many scientists believe … (Is it just the writer's opinion? Who believe so? Scientists. Yes.)

T: (write the structure on the blackboard) What's the benefit of citing the scientists' belief?

Ss: Make the reason more acceptable?

T: We can support our point with some reliable details. It will make our writing more acceptable.

2. Read the reason why water is important in paragraph 3 carefully and appreciate how the writer shows the close relation between water and life logically.

T: From the reading, we know there is a close relation between water and life. Please read the reason carefully and circle the key words which can show their relation.

S1: … allow.

T: What does the word mean?

S2: … (make it possible).

T: It is a verb showing effect. Can you find more similar words in these sentences?

Ss: … "produce, make … possible".

T: What's the benefit of using these verbs?

Ss: To state the relation more clearly.

T: In other words, more logically.

3. Read paragraph 4 and judge whether it is developed logically.

T: Thanks to water, plants and animals came into being step by step. What are they?

Ss: …

T: Are they closely related to each other?

Ss: Yes.

T: Does the writer show the relations in a logical way? Read this paragraph and make your judgment.

T: In what order is this paragraph written? (time)

How does the writer show the order clearly? (then, next, after that)

Actually, these are called discourse markers. What's the benefit of using these markers?

Ss: To make the writing logical.

T: The writer presents the development of plants and animals by using some discourse markers to show the time order and some words: e.g. "encourage, follow, make … possible" to show their close relation.

【设计说明】 引导学生在进一步理解文本的基础上赏析作者的写作手法。通过研读第三段,学生发现作者引用科学家的观点来阐述水对生命起源的重要性。然后通过聚焦科学家的观点,学生找出能够阐明水和生命起源之间关系的词或词组如 allow, produce 和 make... possible。接着学生通过领会 allow 和 produce 表示"促使"和"使……产生"的意思,体会作者措辞的严谨。紧接着学生从措辞角度去阅读第四段发现并积累更多表示关系的词如 encourage 和 follow,同时又能够体会语篇衔接词增强文章逻辑性作用。本环节的三个活动层层递进,是从理解到赏析再到初步运用的过程。

Step 3. Commenting on the writing skills

Read Para. 5 and judge whether the writer states the influence of humans on the earth in a reasonable and logical way.

T: Does the writer develop the idea in a logical and reasonable way?

S: The writer makes the statement reasonable by quoting what scientists believe and develops the theme logically by using some discourse markers such as "thus, but, as a result of this".

【设计说明】 该任务旨在帮助学生初步运用在第三、四段所学的写作技巧来赏析最后一段。学生会发现作者不仅用了科学家的观点作为地球变暖的现象的依据,使其叙述较为可信。同时也用了一些语篇衔接词如 thus, but 和 as a result of this 来说明温室效应的前因后果来增强论述的逻辑性。

Step 4. Exploring the writer's writing purpose

Discuss with partners why the writer writes about global warming in the last paragraph under the theme of the beginning of life.

T: Why is the global warming mentioned here?

Ss: ...

T: In conclusion, the writer intends to stress the close relation between humans and the future of life on the earth so as to arouse readers' awareness of protecting the earth.

【设计说明】 通过引导学生思考第四段大意和全文主题的关系来培养学生的批判性思维。同时,学生通过聚焦作者温室效应的态度,挖掘作者的写作意图,理解人类活动与地球生存息息相关,增强环境保护意识。

Step 5. Applying the writing skills

Brainstorm some suggestions on solving the problem of global warming and then write down a few reasonable suggestions in a logical way by using the newly-learnt writing skills.

T: What can we do to solve this problem? Think of suggestions as many as possible.

Ss: Save paper/save energy (e. g. electricity)/plant more trees/use public transportation/

develop green energy . . .

T：You came up with so many suggestions. Why can they work? You are supposed to offer the reason why your suggestions can work. Please write it down and organize your words logically.

【设计说明】 通过提出解决温室效应的措施,运用在课文中提炼出来的写作技巧来表述自己的建议,达到落实巩固课堂教学内容的目的,最终完成本堂课从理解到赏析再到运用的全过程。

2. 板书设计

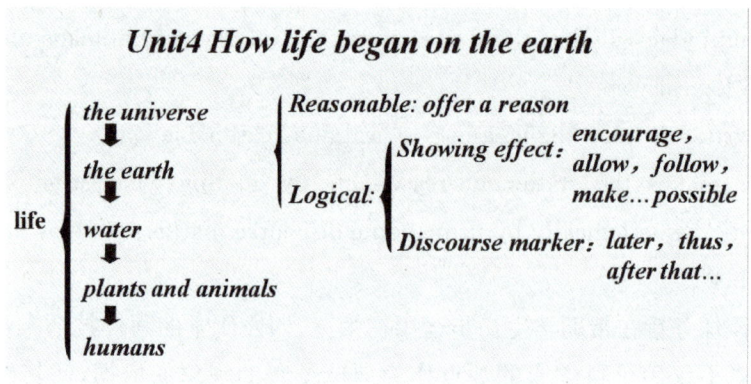

3. 作业布置

Improve your report by checking the following points：

❖ Do I give a reasonable suggestion?
❖ Do I present my suggestions in a logical way?

(三) 教学反思

通过本节课的学习,学生不仅加深了对文本的理解,而且学习了写作技巧,并能够在新语境中初步运用该技巧。笔者认为目标达成的主要原因有以下三点：

1. 立足文本学习语言,促进文本的深层次理解

在本节课中,笔者将学生对语篇的深层理解与体会写作技巧两者有机结合,通过一定的活动使学生在感知语言中进一步体会作者的意图,在加深对文本的理解的同时操练并运用语言。例如,通过聚焦表现物种起源连锁反应的动词 allow 和 encourage 等,巩固了学生对物种起源过程的理解,明白物种起源和环境息息相关。又如,通过提炼 as a result 等表示因果的语篇连接词,学生进一步挖掘气候变暖的原因,从而理解作者的写作意图。

2. 设计语言赏析活动,激发学生语言运用的主动性

语言学习是阅读第二课时的一个重点,然而有时候学生学习了词汇的用法后,虽然知道了怎么用,但却不知道何时用或为何用。因此笔者认为在引导学生理解语言的意义和用法的同时,应该引导学生关注语言的精妙运用,从而激发学生学习语言的兴趣和动力。如在第

一次试讲中,笔者仅仅提炼了三个目标句型,但没有引导学生感知该句型的运用的闪光点,然后在后面的改写练习中直接要求学生用上句型。虽然个别学生能准确改写,但是他们只是被动地运用,并没有真正内化。本节课中,教师在提炼句型后引导学生对比赏析,在此基础上,在后面改写任务中笔者只是要求他们将语言润色,虽然没有明确要求他们运用这些句型,学生也能够主动有效地运用目标句型,可见赏析语言的重要性。

3. 创设新语境,升华情感目标并促成熟词新用

阅读第二课时要从文本出发,但不能止于文本,教师要创设新语境使学生能够将本课的所学的语言和写作技巧进行初步运用。本节课的最后,在学生解读作者对待环境保护的态度后,笔者选择了如何缓解温室效应话题请学生讨论,加强学生关注环境问题的意识。同时该话题为语言知识的运用提供了较开放的空间,学生可以运用表示因果的语篇衔接词,能够运用本课所学的句型。

(教学设计撰写:温州中学 蔡珍瑞)

教材文本

How Life Began on the Earth

No one knows exactly how the earth began, as it happened so long ago. However, according to a widely accepted theory, the universe began with a "Big Bang" that threw matter in all directions. After that, atoms began to form and combine to create stars and other bodies.

For several billion years after the "Big Bang", the earth was still just a cloud of dust. What it was to become was uncertain until between 4.5 and 3.8 billion years ago when the dust settled into a solid globe. The earth became so violent that it was not clear whether the shape would last or not. It exploded loudly with fire and rock. They were in time to produce carbon, nitrogen, water vapor and other gases, which were to make the earth's atmosphere. What is even more important is that as the earth cooled down, water began to appear on its surface.

Water had also appeared on other planets like Mars but unlike the earth, it had disappeared later. It was not immediately obvious that water was to be fundamental to the development of life. What many scientists believe is that the continued presence of water allowed the earth to dissolve harmful gases and acids into the oceans and seas. This produced a chain reaction, which made it possible for life to develop.

Many millions of years later, the first extremely small plants began to appear on the surface of the water. They multiplied and filled the oceans and seas with oxygen, which encouraged the later development of early shellfish and all sorts of fish. Next, green plants began to grow on land. They were followed in time by land animals. Some were insects. Others, called amphibians, were able to live on land as well as in the water. Later when the plants grew into forests, reptiles appeared for the first time. They produced young generally by laying eggs. After that, some huge animals, called dinosaurs, developed. They laid eggs too and existed on the earth for more than 140 million years. However, 65 million years ago the age of the dinosaurs ended. Why they suddenly disappeared still remains a mystery. This disappearance made possible the rise of mammals on the earth. These animals were different from all life forms in the past, because they gave birth to young baby animals and produced milk to feed them.

Finally about 2.6 million years ago some small clever animals, now with hands and feet, appeared and spread all over the earth. Thus they have, in their turn, become the most important animals on the planet. But they are not looking after the earth very well. They are putting too much carbon dioxide into the atmosphere, which prevents heat from escaping from the earth into space. As a result of this, many scientists believe the earth may become too hot to live on. So whether life will continue on the earth for millions of years to come will depend on whether this problem can be solved.

说课案例三（阅读课）

PEP NSEFC M1 U5 Elias' story (Reading)

Good morning, ladies and gentlemen! I'm XX from XXXX. It is my honor to present my lesson here. The lesson is from Unit 5, Module 1, NSEFC, titled *Elias' story*.

1. Analysis

According to the title, we can clearly see that this is a story told by Elias, where we can learn that his life changed because of Mandela. Before meeting Mandela, Elias was a poor black worker who was worried about whether he would become out of work. But luckily, with the guidance of Mandela, he became hopeful towards life. That is to say, without Mandela, Elias was a life sufferer, but luckily, with Mandela, he became a follower and then finally he became a fighter struggling for the equality between the black and the white. At the same time, Mandela's identity also changed. He was not only a helper to Elias, but also a leader who organized the ANC Youth League, and finally he became a mentor for the whole black people. So from the analysis above, we can clearly see that the story has a very clear main clue, that is, change.

About the students, they are in senior one, from Wenzhou No. 2 High School. At this age, the students are interested in reading stories. But because of their limited vocabulary, and immature reading strategies, most of them can only have a literal understanding of the passage, let alone reading between lines or reading beyond lines. Thus some students may have difficulty in understanding the intention of Mandela's words and inferring the changes of both Elias and Mandela.

II. Teaching objectives

Based on the analysis above, here comes my teaching objectives. Firstly, with the help of the context, the students will be able to guess the meaning of certain words, such as "stage" and "position" and then interpret the intention of Mandela's words. Secondly, with the understanding of the details about what happened to the two characters, the students will be able to summarize the changes of Elias and Mandela. Thirdly, by choosing the best title of the story, the students' ability in critical thinking can be developed.

III. Description

In my reading class, I will lead the students to achieve all those objectives and deal with the difficulties in the following teaching procedure. The procedure consists of 5 activities. As the class goes on, the comprehension difficulty increases gradually.

Activity one is lead-in and scanning. According to the title, the students can tell that the type of writing is a story. I'll ask the students the basic elements of a story. They are "who", "when", "where", "why", "what", and "how". After activating the their previous knowledge about a narrative writing, the students will have about 30 seconds to scan Paragraph One and locate the basic elements in Elias' story.

After finding out the basic elements in the story, the students will have a prediction of the end of the story, which is Activity 2. Based on information in Paragraph One, the students may come up with the following answers. Maybe Elias will become a successful black leader like Mandela. Or maybe he will become a lawyer. This step can not only stimulate the students' interest in reading the rest part of the story, but also is beneficial to the further reading.

Activity 3 is detailed reading. It is time for the students to check their prediction on their own. I'll ask the students to find out the supporting details about the changes in Elias' feeling. From the reading, they can find some sentences with adjectives describing one's feelings, such as "I was worried about whether I would become out of work", "The day when Nelson Mandela helped me was one of my happiest" and "I became more hopeful about my future". To sum up, the changes of his feeling are from "worried" to "happy" then to "hopeful". However, just summarizing the changes in Elias' feeling is not enough. During the conversation with the student, I will ask the following questions: "What caused the changes in his feeling?", "How did Elias feel to the guidance of Mandela?" and "What did Elias do to convey his gratitude to Mandela?" After answering this series of questions, the students may gradually realize another change of Elias. That is the changes in Elias's identity. Actually Elias was no longer a life sufferer, but become brave and finally he turned to a fighter struggling for the equality between the black and the white.

However, these changes would not have happened without Mandela's guidance, so in Activity 4 — deep understanding, I'll lead the students to turn their attention from Elias to Mandela. I will ask them whether Mandela's identity changed during the process. After reading, discussing and analyzing, the students may realize actually Mandela's identity also changed. He was not only a helper but also a leader and a mentor for all the black people. Then I'll ask the students "What kind of role did Mandela play?" The answer lies in Mandela's words. Some students may have difficulty in understanding the long sentences, so I will make full use of the context to help them guess the meaning of certain words, such as "stage" and "position". Here these two words mean "situation". After literal understanding, I'll lead the students to understand the intention of Mandela's words. Actually, Mandela not only analyzed the current situation the black people were facing but also pointed out the solutions including the ways to fight against the government and the attitude to the fighting ways.

Step 5 is an after-reading activity, which is aimed at training the students' critical thinking. I will give students three different titles — *Elias' story*, *Mandela's story* and *The changes of a black worker*. The students are required to make their choices of the best title according to their understanding and then state their reasons. The intention of this activity is to create an open platform where the students can share their voices bravely and freely, so any answer will be accepted and appreciated as long as it is reasonable.

Ⅳ. Exposition

At the end of this lesson comes the homework. I will ask the students to write a letter. Suppose they were Elias, and they are going to write a letter to Mandela to express their gratitude to the great leader and to praise the great influence of Mandela. The letter should be written within 100 words.

Let's come to the blackboard design. I make use of the notes on board to highlight the main clue — change. The mind map not only reflects the changes of Elias and Mandela in a concrete way, but also clearly shows the great influence of Mandela in each period. Besides, with the words on the blackboard, the students can reinforce the vocabulary at the same time.

Ⅴ. Reflection

To sum up, this lesson has a clear clue, that is, change. As the class goes on, the students will have a deeper understanding of the passage, from literal reading, to interpretive reading and finally to critical reading. During this process, the students not only enjoy the story, know some words, but also their abilities in interpreting, analyzing and critical thinking can be well practiced. That's all for my presentation. Thanks for listening.

（说课稿撰写：温州第二高级中学　余依晨）

 附：教学设计及教材文本

M1 U5 Elias' story

（一）教学分析

1. 教材分析

本课教材选自人教版《普通高中课程标准实验教科书英语必修1》第五单元，阅读材料选自 Reading 部分——Elias' story，是一篇故事类叙事文。叙事者 Elias 初次见到 Mandela 时，是个陷入生活困境的黑人少年，正是在 Mandela 的帮助下，获得了在城市继续工作的合法权利，对生活再次燃起希望。他对 Mandela 的善良无私一直感激在心，此后积极参加 Mandela 引导的反政府活动，为争取获得黑人的平等权利而战斗。

本文故事情节连贯，清晰完整。虽然围绕英雄话题，但有别于惯常采用的平铺直叙方

式，而是以普通人视角，讲述发生在身边和 Mandela 相关的故事，从侧面反映出 Mandela 的领袖作用，读起来更加亲切真实，可读性强。

文章在叙事的同时，穿插了 Mandela 讲话的内容。直接引语部分多为长难句，从词句角度分析，句中含有一词多义，在特定的语境中被赋予新含义，例如 stage 和 position，可通过上下文猜测词义；其次，涵盖丰富的句子类型，包括抽象名词作为先行词，引导的定语从句，部分倒装句等，均应成为学生品读赏析的语句。此外，话语背后还体现了人物的作用，在词句字面含义疏通后，教师应启发学生思考，深入理解话语意图。

2. 学生分析

授课对象为高一学生，处于高中语言学习的过渡阶段。该阶段的学生对故事类体裁的文章兴趣浓厚，但词汇量有限、阅读策略和语篇分析能力不够健全，导致部分学生只能进行低水平的认知性阅读，而对深层次的理解性阅读和批判性阅读则浅尝辄止，即学生分析、概括、筛选、推敲、评价阅读材料的能力偏弱。

此外，据课前情况了解，大部分学生对于主人公之一的 Mandela 的认知，仅限于黑人领袖，对本文故事发生背景，即 20 世纪五六十年代的黑人处境也较为陌生。背景知识的欠缺，在一定程度上增加了学生阅读理解的难度。

3. 教学目标

1) 语言能力与学习能力

能够借助上下文语境，推测词义，理解 stage 和 position 等词汇一词多义的用法，进而理解 Mandela 的说话意图，并推敲其在文中的作用。

2) 文化意识与思维品质

通过体裁特征预测文本，聚焦关键词"change"，归纳人物性格与身份变化；通过深入挖掘文本，了解黑人的历史处境，并评价 Mandela 在黑人获取平等权利过程中的重要作用；通过评价标题反思文本写作特色，重在训练理解性思维和批判性思维。

4. 教学重难点

本课教学重点为归纳遇见 Mandela 前后，Elias 发生的种种变化，要求学生围绕核心"change"，捕捉、提炼关键词句。学生需要在大篇幅的叙事情节中，梳理出 Elias 不同方面的具体变化，包括情绪、身份等。再类比 Elias 的改变，梳理出在此过程中，Mandela 对于 Elias 而言身份上的改变。

本节课的难点为阐释文中 Mandela 的话语意图，评价他作为伟大黑人领袖的历史作用，并在学习全文后，运用批判性思维，选择自己认为的最佳标题，提出自己的思考与见解。

5. 教学思路

基于文本分析，教师抓住本文故事的核心"change"，从故事入手，在梳理文章的内容的基础上，引导归纳 Elias 和 Mandela 在人物性格与身份上的变化。通过阅读课上设计的教学问题,顺应布鲁姆的六大认知目标。即知道、领会、应用、分析、综合和评价,引导学生一步步进行认知性阅读、理解性阅读和批判性阅读,从易到难,逐步推进对学生思维能力的训练。

本节课共包括三大教学步骤。步骤一,开门见山——认知性思维与阅读,带领学生回顾故事类文章的基本组成要素,并快速阅读文章第一段,获取本文对应的基本要素,即 who、when、where 和 what,简单梳理故事背景框架;再基于已知故事背景和人物关系,引出本文主线——change,预测下文故事发展的结局。步骤二,循序渐进——理解性思维与阅读,阅读过程聚焦核心 change,要求学生梳理 Elias 发生的变化,提炼文章细节,或用自己的语言进行概括。同时思考,发生改变的原因是什么。在这过程中,另一个故事主人公,Mandela 的身份同时发生哪些转变,进而解读长难句部分——Mandela 的直接引语,包括语言层面、内容层面。步骤三,水到渠成——批判性思维和阅读,综合故事的内容和主旨,在教师给出的三个文章标题中,选择最佳标题,并陈述理由。

(二) 教学过程

1. 教学活动

步骤一. 开门见山——认知性思维与阅读

Activity One: Lead-in & scanning (10 mins)

Activate the previous knowledge about the basic elements of a narration with questions and then scan Paragraph One to locate the basic information.

T: Morning, everyone. Today we are going to read a passage titled *Elias' story*. What are the basic elements of a story?

Ss: Who/When/Where/What/Why/How.

T: Yes. Now turn to page 43. Scan Paragraph One quickly and locate these basic elements.

Ss: (silent reading)

T: Any one can tell me where the story happened?

S1: In the South Africa.

T: Who are the characters in the story?

S1: Elias and Mandela.

T: What happened between Elias and Mandela?

S2: Elias went to Mandela for help.

S3: Mandela offered guidance to Elias.

T: What did Mandela help Elias do?

S4: Mandela helped Elias solve legal problems.

T: So what was the relationship between them?

S5: A Lawyer and a poor black worker.

T: Yes, but actually, to Elias, Mandela was more than a lawyer. He was a . . . ?

Ss: Helper.

T: Great!

【设计意图】 本节课的阅读材料文体十分明显,是故事题材。开门见山,直接关注阅读体裁,激活学生对于叙事类文章基本元素的已有知识,很自然引出叙事部分的 when、where 和 who 等浅层次信息。学生扫读文章第一段,定位、提取对应内容,不需要对信息加工。该活动旨在训练学生的认知性思维,用以检查他们对故事背景的掌握情况,为之后的教学活动铺垫信息基础。

Activity Two: Prediction (3 mins)

Make a prediction about the ending of Elias' story based on the beginning of the story.

T: What kind of life did Elias live when he first met Mandela?

Ss: A poor life. /He was in a very difficult period of life.

T: Yes, that was his life before meeting Mandela. But then after he met Mandela, do you think his life would still be as suffering as before?

Ss: No.

T: Can you make a bold prediction about the ending of Elias' story?

Ss: (Think)

T: The story begins with his suffering boyhood. How about the end?

S6: Maybe he would become a successful black leader like Mandela.

T: Wow! What an amazing ending! Any reason?

S6: Because Elias looked up to Mandela. Mandela was his hero.

T: I see. The hero effect turned Elias into a black leader too. How about others?

S7: With the guidance of Mandela, Elias became a lawyer.

T: You think he might be a lawyer. Why?

S7: Because once Mandela helped the poor black solve legal problems. Maybe after that Elias realized the importance of legal knowledge.

T: That sounds very reasonable. It seems that we all agree that after meeting Mandela, Elias' life was different. So what might have Mandela done to him?

S8: He has changed Elias.

T: Great! Do you want to know the changes in detail? Now continue reading the rest of the story.

【设计意图】 本教学步骤让学生根据故事开篇的基本信息,先对故事结局进行自我预测,然后再自己去验证预测。从教师的追问可以看出,学生的预测不是盲目的,而是基于文本信息展开的有理有据的推理。根据第一段内容,学生不难预测出故事肯定存在转折,Elias 会因为 Mandela 的引导而发生改变。在该教学步骤的设计,不仅留下悬念,激发学生的阅读兴趣,而且有助于学生的理解性思维培养。

步骤二. 循序渐进——理解性思维与阅读

Activity One: Detailed reading — summarize the changes of Elias (10 mins)

Continue reading the rest part of the story to find the supporting details that show the changes in Elias's feelings. And some questions aimed at detailed understanding are added. With the guidance of these questions, the students will summarize another change in Elias — identity.

T: Have you finished your reading?

Ss: Yes.

T: Have you found any changes in Elias' feeling?

S9: Before meeting Mandela, Elias was worried about whether he would be out of work. But, in line 15, his feeling changed. "The day when Nelson Mandela helped me was one of my happiest." And "I became more hopeful about my future."

T: Very good. Can you summarize the changes in feelings with different adjectives?

S9: (Thinking)

T: You can use the words in the text or your own words.

S9: From hopeless to hopeful.

T: Good job! (Note on the blackboard)

T: Why was Elias hopeless before meeting Mandela? What was he worried about?

S10: He might be out of job.

T: What does "out of job" mean?

S10: He might lose his job.

T: Why would he lose his job?

S11: Because he didn't have Mandela's help?

T: How did he feel toward Mandela?

S12: Grateful.

T: Did Elias do something to show his gratitude to Mandela?

S13: Yes.

T: What did Elias do then?

S14: When Mandela organized ANC Youth League, he joined it as soon as he could.

T: Which phrase especially shows his gratitude?

S14: "As soon as I could".

T: Yes.

T: Well done. What else did Elias do?

S15: In 1963 Elias helped Mandela blow up some government buildings.

T: That sounds quite dangerous. Why would he do that?

S15: Because it would help achieve the dream of making black and white people equal.

T: Great! Thank you. Now let's go back to the beginning of the story. At first, he suffered a lot in his miserable life, so we can say he was a...?

Ss: Sufferer.

T: Yes! (Note on the blackboard) Then he met Mandela, and with the guidance of Mandela, he followed Mandela to join in the ANC Youth League. At that time, he became a?

Ss: Follower.

T: You guys are very clever. (Note on the blackboard) How about the end? He fought for the equality of the black.

Ss: Fighter.

T: So these reflect the changes in...?

S16: His identity.

T: You got it!

【设计说明】 该教学环节聚焦"change"一词,重在前后信息对比,而且是基于表层信息的加工。叙事部分学生无阅读障碍,但是"change"是一个很宽泛的词,而 Elias 产生的改变也是多方面的,需要学生找到分散在文章前后的支撑细节后,用高度概括的词汇提炼出一条变化线索。在理解性思维阅读步骤中,应当给学生提供足够的沉默阅读时间,教师应该做的是耐心等待。只有在充分的语言输入和内化的基础上,才能激发高质量的思维输出。在阅读过程中,借助原文中 worried、happy 和 hopeful 这些标志性的形容词,学生最容易找出的是 feeling 上的改变,并梳理出情感主线变化。恰巧,该主线又能用来串联整篇故事,值得充分挖掘。在师生问答过程中,教师不断通过逻辑紧密的追问,同时在黑板上记录下关键信息,推动学生对人物的研读和对主题"the change of Elias"的深入挖掘,引导学生树立语篇整体意识,进而归纳出 the change in identity,即 sufferer — follower — fighter。这一过程,不仅帮助学生充分理解故事情节,同时为学生充分理解作为黑人领袖的 Mandela 对当时黑人群体产生的巨大影响作铺垫。

Activity Two: Comprehensive reading — the changes in Mandela's identities (12 mins)

Summarize Mandela's changes in identity during the process. Then with the help of context, the students guess the meaning of certain words such as "stage", "position", then interpret the intention of Mandela's words and appreciate the great influence of the famous black leader.

T: However, the great changes of Elias would not have happened without Mandela. Do you think Mandela's identity also changed during the process? Read the passage once again.

Ss: (Read silently)

T: In the beginning, when Elias was worried about being out of work, what did Mandela do?

Ss: Helped Elias.

S17: Helper.

T: That's it. Then why did Elias join the ANC Youth League?

S18: Because Mandela organized the organization.

T: So at that time Mandela became a?

S18: Leader.

T: Why did Mandela organize ANC Youth League?

S19: Because the black people were treated unequally.

T: That was the situation of the black. (Note on the blackboard). Can you give some supporting details?

S20: "The greatest number of laws stopping their rights and progress".

T: Where do you find the information?

S20: From Mandela's words.

T: OK. Let's read Mandela's quotation together.

Ss: (Read loudly together)

T: How do you feel after reading?

S21: I feel pity on them and feel angry toward the government.

T: Why?

S21: Because the black had been treated unequally for 30 years.

T: You focus on the long time. How do you understand the word "stage" here?

S22: (Thinking)

T: Never mind. Let's see who have some ideas?

S23: Situation.

T: Yes, the word on board. Do you all agree?

Ss: Yes.

T: Considering the situation of the black, Elias joined the organization. What did he do?

S24: He blew up some government buildings.

T: Was he willing to do that? It was very dangerous.

Ss: Yes.

T: Why?

S25: To achieve their dream of making black and white equal.

T: What kind of role did Mandela play during the process?

S26: Guider.

T： Especially a guider in spirit. That is called "mentor". So what are the changes in Mandela's identity?

Ss： Helper-leader-mentor.

T： Great! Mandela's quotation is quite long, but what did he want to stress?

S27： He stressed the unequal situation the blacks were facing.

T： Yes. Then what did he suggest?

S28： They should fight against the government.

T： How to fight? In what way?

S29： They first broke the law in a way which was peaceful. When it failed, they would do it in violence.

【设计说明】 这部分的核心依旧围绕 change, 只是目光转向 Mandela 的身份改变。学生类比 Elias 在三个时期的不同变化, 分别用一个词归纳出 Mandela 在不同时期身份的转变。此外, 部分学生可能难以充分理解文中引号部分的 Mandela 原话, 教师可充分借助语境, 让学生对 stage 和 position 二词进行猜测。同时, 引导学生思考话中为何特地强调时间, 进而解读 Mandela 的说话意图。本环节的教学活动难度大、要求高, 学生的理解性思维参与度大。阅读不再局限于语码的解读, 更是阅读文字背后深意, 体会 Mandela 的伟人领袖作用。

步骤三. 水到渠成——批判性思维与阅读

Activity: Critical thinking — the best title (5 mins)

Discuss in groups and choose from the three given titles, "*Elias' story*", "*Mandela's story*", and "*The change of a black worker*".

T： Now we've finished reading the whole story. What does the story tell you? Can you use one sentence?

S30： Elias' life was greatly changed with the guidance of Mandela.

T： Very brief and to the point. Now let's go back to the title. The title is?

Ss： Elias' story.

T： Well, what do you think of the title? Here I offer you three different options of titles *Elias' story*, *Mandela's story*, and *The change of a black worker*. Which one do you prefer? Discuss in groups.

Ss： (Think and discuss)

T： Anyone would like to share your preference?

G1： Our group prefers *Elias' story*. Because Mandela is a famous person. There are already many stories about him. If I read the title *Mandela's story*, I may not want to read it.

T： So you agree with the story writer. How about others? Any different ideas?

G2: We think *Mandela's story* is better. Without Mandela, Elias' life wouldn't be like this. It was Mandela who affected him a lot and caused the great change.

T: That sounds very reasonable. Any group prefers *The change of a black worker*?

G3: We choose *The change of a black worker*. Because "change" is the focus of this story. And I think Elias represents thousands of suffering poor black workers. This title is more meaningful.

T: Thank you for your wonderful idea! I really appreciate all your ideas. Though different, they all sound very persuasive. Good job!

【设计说明】 教师在前面的教学步骤中,已经带领学生进行认知性思维阅读和理解性思维阅读。最后一个步骤设计的思维训练旨在调动学生在之前叙事阅读活动中所有的收获和思考,将阅读任务升级至评论层次,锻炼学生的批判性思维。通过给学生三个不同的标题选择,让学生基于自己的理解和阅读体验,选择出一个最合适的标题。在这个过程中,学生不仅能提高独立思考能力,而且能建立自身逻辑的思辨。教师需要及时给予学生积极的评价,肯定学生创造性的思考成果。让学生体会到阅读过程中,多元思维碰撞带来的乐趣,同时鼓励学生学会站在不同视角看待问题。

2. 板书设计

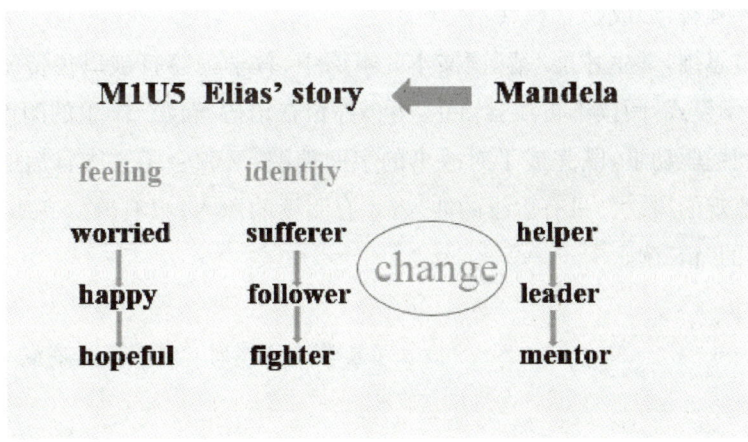

3. 作业布置

Practical Writing:

Suppose you were Elias, please write a letter (about 80 words) to Mandela to express your gratitude to him.

(三) 教学反思

1. 教学活动重层次,"厚"读文本

教师教学活动的设计,应当顺应学生的思维模式,由浅入深,呈递进式,尽可能使更多的

学生能参与到课堂教学中来。本堂阅读课，教学活动重层次。随着学生阅读的深入，教学活动难度层次和开放程度逐渐递增。步骤一难度较低，问题皆是封闭式的，面向全体学生。步骤二先是难度中等的封闭式问题，再是难度较高半开放式问题，学生只有在前一环节的基础上，才能稳步推进后一环节。步骤三为开放式问题，难度虽然较大，但是在前面两步的铺垫之下，本来无法完成任务的后进生也能勇于一试。

教学活动重层次，学生才能读"厚"文本。本课中，教学设问从展示性问题，到参阅性问题，再到最终的评估性问题，学生既完成了文本语言的字面含义的解读，赏读了一篇启人心智的故事；又品鉴了作者的措辞造句，分析、评价、赏析了文字的语用功能，训练了阅读技巧，提高了阅读能力；还通过阅读，了解了一段文化，品读了一则故事，领略了一个伟人。教学活动是"外在"，学生的所得就是"内在"。只有层次化的教学活动，才有文本的"厚"读。

2. 教学内容重思维，"精"读文本

教学内容的设计，应当推动学生阅读的深入，从涉及低层次思维的阅读，逐步过渡到高层次思维的阅读，既要注重文字的记忆与理解，也留有独立思维的自由创造空间，还鼓励学生创造性思辨。本堂阅读课，教学活动重思维。学生一读文章，重在认知性思维，疏通故事大意；二读文章，基于理解性思维，深入文本，以简要的文字，提炼概括故事主线，解读作者言下之意，体会写作意图；三读文章，旨在批判性思维，以审辩的目光思考原文标题得当与否，基于文本的深入理解，形成独立观点。

教学内容重思维，学生才能"精"读文本。本课中，教学内容打破以往传统阅读教学"走马观花"式的教学模式，阅读不再浅尝辄止，不再停留在语码解读。学生的阅读深入浅出，在教师高质量的问题驱动下，既完成了对故事的字面理解，又领会了文本背后的思想情感，树立了正确的价值观的树立。只有思维的涉入，才有阅读的深入；只有融入高质量思维的教学内容，才有文本的"精"读。

（教学设计撰写：温州第二高级中学　余依晨）

教材文本

Elias' story

My name is Elias. I am a poor black worker in South Africa. The time when I first met Nelson Mandela was a very difficult period of my life. I was twelve years old. It was in 1952 and Mandela was the black lawyer to whom I went for advice. He offered guidance to poor black people on their legal problems. He was generous with his time, for which I was grateful.

I needed his help because I had very little education. I began school at six. The school where I studied for only two years was three kilometers away. I had to leave because my family could not continue to pay the school fees and the bus fare. I could not read or write well. After trying hard, I got a job in a gold mine. However, this was a time when one had got to have a passbook to live in Johannesburg. Sadly I did not have it because I was not born there, and I worried about whether I would become out of work.

The day when Nelson Mandela helped me was one of my happiest. He told me how to get the correct papers so I could stay in Johannesburg. I became more hopeful about my future. I never forgot how kind Mandela was. When he organized the ANC Youth League, I joined it as soon as I could. He said:

"The last thirty years have seen the greatest number of laws stopping out rights and progress, until today we have reached a stage where we have almost no rights at all."

It was the truth. Black people could not vote or choose their leaders. They could not get the jobs they wanted. The parts of town in which they had to live were decided by white people. The places outside the towns where they were sent to live were the poorest parts of South Africa. No one could grow food there. In fact as Nelson Mandela said:

"... we were put into a position in which we had either to accept we were less important or fight the government. We chose to attack the laws. We first broke the law in a way which was peaceful; when this was not allowed ... only then did we decide to answer violence with violence."

As a matter of fact, I do not like violence ... but in 1963 I helped him blow up some government buildings. It was very dangerous because if I was caught I could be put in prison. But I was happy to help because I knew it would help us achieve our dream of making black and white people equal.

 说课案例四（阅读课）

PEP NSEFC M2 U3 Computers(Reading)

Good afternoon, everyone! I'm XX from XXXX. It's my great honor to stand here to present my lesson plan to you. The lesson I am going to talk about is reading from Unit 3 Module 2, NSEFC.

I. Analysis

The topic of Unit 3 is computers and the title of the reading passage is *Who am I?*. The content of the reading passage is about the development of computers and their applications. There are some difficult vocabulary in the passage such as *calculating machine*, *artificial intelligence* and so on. But this problem will be solved in students' preview work. The structure of each paragraph in this passage is clear. Each paragraph has a topic sentence and supporting details. And the topic sentences of these three paragraphs are all the first sentences. So, students have no difficulty in finding out the topic sentences since they are very obvious. But their ability to analyze the structure of the whole paragraph is still to be improved. There are two ways of organizing the details in this passage, which is also a challenging task for them to distinguish and appreciate.

II. Statement

According to the analysis of the teaching material and students' learning conditions, I set the following learning objectives. First, by the end of the lesson, students will be able to know about the development of computers and their applications; recognize and understand related vocabulary, such as *simplify*, *sum*, *application* and so on; they will be able to know the main idea of the whole passage and each paragraph and detailed information of a paragraph using predicting, skimming and scanning. Second, students will be able to analyze the structure of a paragraph, tell the topic sentence, find out the detailed information and the way these details are organized, which will be the important points of today's lesson. Third, students will be able to form a correct viewpoint of how the development of computers and applications influence human beings.

During students' learning process, it may be difficult for them to analyze the structure of the whole paragraph and figure out how the detailed information is organized.

III. Description

With the help of multimedia and PPT, students' learning objectives will be achieved in the following procedure.

Step One: Warming-up (3 mins). First, students will talk about what they know about computers and then look at the pictures on Page 17 and tell what these pictures show them. From these seven pictures students are expected to tell the development of technology and computers. And the words in the last picture "What's next?" can greatly activate their imaginative thinking.

Step two: Predicting (2 mins). Before reading, students are asked to predict who the speaker "I" is and the main idea of the passage according to the the title and the two pictures in the reading passage. The application of personification in the title *"Who am I?"* can arouse students' curiosity and interest in reading.

Step three: Fast-reading (7 mins). Next, students will read the passage, check their prediction and answer three questions using key words.

Questions: 1. Who is the speaker "I"?

2. What's the the main idea of the whole passage?

3. What's the main idea of each paragraph?

After reading, they can understand the passage and find the answer easily. The main idea of the passage is "the development of computers and applications". And the main ideas of each paragraph are as follows. Paragraph 1 is about the change of computers. Paragraph 2 is about the improvement of memory. Paragraph 3 is about applications of computers. Then I will ask a question "How can you find out the main idea of each paragraph so quickly" to lead them to focus on the topic sentences and discuss their functions.

Step four: Careful reading (23 mins). The next step includes three activities to deal with details of three paragraphs respectively.

Activity one: Reading and discovering — Para. 1 (10 mins). First, students will read paragraph 1 and find out *"How has the computer been changed over time?"* and fill in the blanks in a table including "when", "what was the computer called" and "its characteristics". During the process, some related words such as *simplify difficult sums* will be dealt with. Students are asked to explain these words in English according to the context. After that, I will ask them to use one word to summarize the details in the table. Students will find the answer is "change", which is also the key word of the topic sentence in paragraph 1. So they can find the function of these details is to support and clarify the topic sentence. Next, I will ask a question *"How are these details organized in Paragraph 1?"* After reading, they will find these details are connected by some linking words such as *as time went by*, *from then on* and so on and the details are organized in time order. Finally, a conclusion will be drawn here — in a paragraph there is a topic sentence and supporting details, and all the details are organized logically with the help of linking words.

Activity two: Reading and practicing — Para. 2 (7 mins). Next they are going to use what have learned in Paragraph 1 to analyze the structure of Paragraph 2. First they will read and then they will discuss in groups. After reading and discussing, students are expected to find out the details in Paragraph 2 are also organized in time order using linking words such as *first*, *then*, *later*. Then I will ask students the question *"Why did 'I' say*

'*These changes only became possible as my memory improved?*'" to guide students to focus on the relationship between these two paragraphs and then conclude that the first sentence pf Paragraph 2 is not only the topic sentence but also serves as the transitional sentence between Paragraph 1 and Paragraph 2. By doing this, students are guided to focus on the logic between sentences and paragraphs.

Activity three: Reading and using — Para. 3 (6 mins). Now they are asked to use the skills they have learned in Paragraph 1 and Paragraph 2 to analyze the structure of Paragraph 3 by themselves. After reading and analyzing, the students are expected to find the linking words *and*, *also*, *as well as*, *even* and tell that the details are organized in the way of listing, and figure out the last two sentences are not supporting details of the topic sentence but a conclusion.

Activity four: Thinking and discussing (5 mins). After reading, the students are asked to discuss in groups about the question "What do you think of the development of computers?" They can have their opinions but they should give details to support their ideas. During the discussion, students' ability of creative thinking will be enhanced and hopefully, they can form a correct viewpoint about this topic.

IV. Exposition

After discussion, a writing task will be given to enhance what they have learned today as homework. They are asked to write a paragraph about what they have discussed just now with a topic sentence and supporting details connected logically with proper linking words.

That's all about the teaching procedure. Now let's look at the blackboard. The learning objectives and important points of today's lesson are presented clearly on the blackboard. With the help of the blackboard, the students will be clearer about the main idea of the passage, the main idea of each paragraph, the structure of a paragraph and the way the details are organized.

V. Reflection

To sum up, different reading tasks are designed to achieve learning objectives and emphasize the important points. During the process, students' ability of analyzing the structure of a paragraph and their awareness of deconstructing a passage will be enhanced. Meanwhile, students' creative thinking and logical thinking abilities are also strengthened.

That's all for my lesson plan presentation. Thanks for your attention.

(说课稿撰写：温州第八高级中学　陈学丹)

附：教学设计及教材文本

M2 U3 Computers

(一) 教学分析

1. 教材分析

本课教材选自人教版《普通高中课程标准实验教科书英语必修2》第三单元,单元中心话题为Computers,内容涉及计算机的发展史、计算机的应用、智能机器人等等。本课阅读材料为该单元的主课文,属于科普类说明文,文章以第一人称自述了计算机的发展和应用。这种拟人手法使原本抽象的内容变得更为有趣,使得专业性较强的语言也显得浅显易懂。

阅读文章由三段构成,每一段段落结构都非常清晰,由一个主题句加细节信息组成。第一段介绍了计算机的发展演变,第二段讲述了计算机的记忆功能的发展,第三段是关于计算机在各个领域的运用。因此,清晰的段落结构为本文的亮点,也是本堂课的重点所在。

本文中有较多与计算机相关的生词,如 calculating machine、analytical machine、technological revolution、network 和 artificial intelligence。这些专业术语只要求学生掌握中文意思、扫除阅读障碍即可,因此要求学生提前预习,解决专业术语带来的阅读困难。

2. 学生分析

授课对象为高一较高层次班级的学生,具有较好的英语基础和英语学习习惯,基本掌握采用速读把握文章大意的阅读技能,但是作为只有4个月高中学习经历的高一学生来说,分析段落结构的能力还有所欠缺。在一个段落中,如果主题句很明显,学生基本能够顺利找出,但是区分主次、提炼关键信息、自主分析段落结构、分析细节信息之间的衔接和逻辑关系等能力还有待提高。

3. 教学目标

(1) 语言能力与学习能力：通过了解计算机的发展史,认识并理解表达计算机发展及应用方面的词汇,如：simplify、sum 和 application 等；能够通过预测、扫读、跳读等技能,完成寻找主题句和细节信息等不同的要求的阅读活动。

(2) 文化意识与思维品质：能够识辩主题句,并根据主题句中的关键词,分析段落组织形式和逻辑,从而归纳段落大意；能够通过表示时间的信号词识辩主题句与支撑句；能够以辩证的角度正确看待计算机的发展给人类带来的影响。

4. 教学重难点

教学重点：识辩主题句,分析、归纳细节信息组织形式和逻辑,分析段落结构。

教学难点：运用所学技能自主分析段落组织形式和逻辑。

5. 教学思路

整个教学过程由任务驱动，任务的设置有梯度，层层递进，环环相扣。先速读文章，把握文章主旨和段落大意；学生根据关键词定位主题句，总结主题句的功能。在把握主题句的基础上分析段落结构和细节信息的组织方式。设置三个活动，层层推进，引导学生分析并归纳段落结构，并应用所学技能。活动一：阅读和发现。细读第一段，找出细节信息以及细节信息之间的组合方式和逻辑关系，找出连接词。此环节在教师的引导下完成，教师以表格的形式为学生搭建支架，并以问题为引导。活动二：阅读和操练。教师撤脚手架，由学生独立阅读、小组讨论完成第二段的结构分析。任务完成后，教师再次引导学生通过解读第二段的主题句分析第一段和第二段之间的关系，总结该句不仅是第二段的主题句，还在第一段和第二段之间起着承上启下的作用，从而培养学生分析句间逻辑和段落间逻辑的能力。活动三：阅读和应用。学生运用所学的技能，分析第三段的段落结构和组织方式。最后，学生就"*the influence of the development of computers on human beings*"进行讨论，用具体细节支撑自己的观点，激发学生批判性思维和创新思维。讨论的内容以作业的形式进行落实。将自己的观点写成一个段落，要有主题句，并且合理地组织细节信息。

（二）教学过程

1. 教学活动

Step 1：Warming-up (3 mins)

Talk about what they know about computers and then look at the pictures on page 17 and tell what these pictures show us.

T：What do you know about computers?

S1：People use computers every day. They are very convenient.

S2：With the help of computers, we can search for information.

S3：We can connect with people from all over the world.

T：Where are computers frequently used?

Ss：They are used in schools, homes, offices, …

T：Do you know what the first computer looked like?

Ss：(Silent)

T：Look at the pictures on page 17. What do these pictures show us?

S4：The development of the computer.

S5：The computer is becoming smaller.

S6：And faster.

T：Good. The computer is developing very fast. What will happen next?

S7：I think maybe robots will replace human beings.

S8: Computer screens will be everywhere. When you touch the table, it becomes a computer screen. The walls in our classrooms will also serve as computer screens.

T: Very imaginative!

S9: Every family will have a robot in their home. The robot will do all the housework.

T: Impressive! The future is full of possibilities as the technology develops.

【设计意图】 Computer虽然是学生熟悉的话题,但是阅读文本所涉及的内容却有着较强的专业性。因此,在导入部分通过问题和图片启动图式,激活学生已有的知识,打开思维,让学生的思维活跃起来,并激发阅读兴趣。通过自由谈论激发学生对计算机的已有认识,学生能够结合实际生活中对计算机的认识发散思维,激活学生与话题相关的知识储备,为阅读做准备。教材17页的7张图片显示了计算机的发展,直观地展示从算盘到机器人的演变,而第8张图片What's next? 留给学生无限的想象空间,激活学生的思维。学生能结合原有认识展开合理想象,发挥想象力和创造力,培养创新精神。

Step 2: Predicting(2 mins)

Look at the title and the two pictures in the reading passage, and predict who the speaker "I" is and what the passage will be about.

【设计意图】 教师引导学生根据标题和课文中的两幅图片预测叙述者是谁以及文章大意,培养学生在阅读时根据标题和图片预测内容的习惯,引起学生阅读的兴趣。标题 Who am I? 采用问题的形式、第一人称以及拟人的手法,能极大地激发学生的好奇心。结合两幅图片,学生能顺利猜出标题中的I应该是计算机。文中第一幅图是分析机,对应课文第一段。第二幅图片展示了计算机在生活中的应用,对应课文第三段。结合标题和图片对文章内容进行猜测,培养阅读技能,铺垫阅读教学。

Step 3: Fast-reading (7 mins)

Read the passage quickly, check their prediction and answer the following questions. They are asked to use key words to answer the questions.

1. Who is the speaker "I"?
2. What's the passage about?
3. What does each paragraph talk about?

T: Who is the speaker "I"?

Ss: The computer.

T: What's the passage about?

Ss: The development/history of computers. (Note on blackboard)

T: Great. What is each paragraph about? Give me key words.

S10: Para. 1 is about the change of computers. Para. 2 is about the improvement of memory. Para. 3 is about the applications. (Note on blackboard)

T: What does "application" mean? Can you explain it in English?

S10: The applications of computers mean computers are used in different fields in our life.

T: Good. (To all the students) Do you agree with him about the main idea of each paragraph?

Ss: Yes.

T: Good. How can you find out the main idea of each paragraph so quickly?

S11: The first sentence.

T: So we call the first sentence the topic sentence. (Note on blackboard) What's the function of a topic sentence?

S12: A topic sentence tells us the main idea of the paragraph.

T: Yes. (To all the students) Is the topic sentence always the first sentence?

Ss: No.

T: Sometimes it can be the ...

Ss: The second sentence, the last sentence ...

T: So we should keep it in mind that the topic sentence should always cover the main idea of a paragraph. After we have a topic sentence, we should give details to support this topic sentence. Now let's focus on the supporting details (Note on blackboard).

【设计意图】 学生带着问题快速阅读文章获取文章大意和各段落大意,并提炼关键词来回答问题。本文段落结构清楚,三个段落的第一句就是主题句。因此,学生能快速、准确定位主题句并提炼出关键词。

Step 4: Careful reading (23 mins)

Activity one: Read and discover — Para. 1 (10 mins)

Read Para. 1 and find out "How has the computer been changed over time?". Use key words to fill in the blanks.

when	what was the computer called	its characteristics
in 1642	calculating machine	simplify difficult sums
It took 200 years before ...	analytical machine	think logically, answer quickly
in 1936	universal machine	solve any ... problem, large in size and brainpower
as time went by, first	PC	made smaller, used in offices and homes
then	laptop	

S13: (Tell when and what the computer was called)

S14: (Tell its characteristics)

T: Can you use one word to summarize the detailed information in this table?

S15: Change.

T: What's the key word in the topic sentence in Para. 1?

S15: Change.

T: So what's the function of the detailed information?

S15: The details are used to support the topic sentence and to make the main idea clearer.

T: Well-done. How are these details organized?

Ss: In the order of time.

T: Good. These details are organized in the order of time by using some linking words. Please find out the words that show us that the change has happened "over time".

Ss: ... began as ... It took 200 years before ... After ... At that time ... In 1936 ... From then on ... By the 1940s ... However ... As time went by ... First ... then ... since 1970s ....

T: Yes. These linking words help connect these details naturally and logically. Let's make a summary. In a paragraph, there is a topic sentence and supporting details, and all the details are organized logically with the help of linking words.

【设计意图】 教师搭建支架,让学生在获取信息的过程中去分析、归纳段落结构以及细节信息的衔接方式。第一段篇幅长、信息量大、生词多,因此教师搭建支架引导学生完成阅读内容,给学生以信心。学生细读第一段,根据表格整理出计算机发展的时间线及不同时期计算机的特点。在学生理解段落内容的基础上,让学生分析表格中的信息,并用一个词来概括和提炼表格所反映的中心思想。学生说出"change"一词,再回到该段主题句中的关键词(change)。细节信息和主题句相匹配,学生就能体会到细节信息在段落中的作用。

理清主题句和细节信息之间的关系后,再引导学生关注细节信息之间的逻辑关系和衔接。学生能快速地读出这些信息是按时间顺序发展的,但是句子与句子之间的衔接却是学生容易忽略的。因此,教师引导学生再读文章,找出用于按时间顺序发展信息的衔接词。最后,对段落结构进行总结。会通过找连接词分析句子之间、段落之间的逻辑关系是一项重要的阅读技能。在写作中能否做到句子之间、段落之间的衔接也是考察学生书面表达能力的一个重要方面。因此,在阅读的过程中培养学生通过找连接词分析细节信息间的逻辑关系的能力显得尤为重要。

Activity two: Read and practise — Para. 2 (7 mins)

1. Read Para. 2 and find out the supporting details and how these details are organized.

2. Work in groups: share their ideas in groups and have a discussion.

T: What details are used to support the topic sentence? How are these details organized? Which group would like to give your answer?

S16: (as the following chart shows)

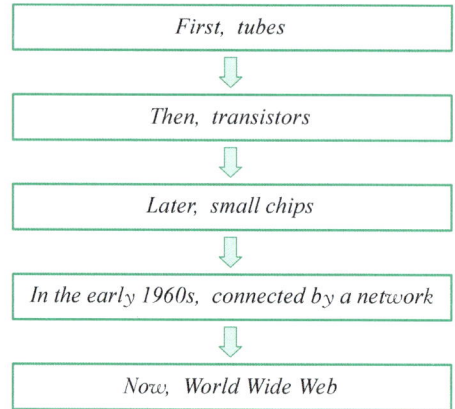

T: Well-done. How are these details organized?

S16: In the order of time. Linking words such as *first*, *then*, *later* are used.

T: Yes. It shows the improvement of its memory. In what way was "my memory" improved?

S17: Smaller in size, larger in memory.

T: What else?

S18: At first every computer worked by itself. Later they were connected by a network so they can share information with others.

T: Good. Smaller in size, larger in memory and connected. Why did "I" say "These changes only became possible as my memory improved"? What do "these changes" refer to?

S19: The changes of computer mentioned in Para. 1. The computer became smaller and more powerful.

T: Good. Why did "I" say "These changes only became possible as my memory improved"?

S19: As time went by, it's memory improved and became powerful. And large memory could be stored in very small chips so the size became smaller. As a result, the computer became smaller and stronger.

T: Very good. So we can know that the first sentence is not only the topic sentence, but also serves as …

S20: The transitional sentence between Para. 1 and Para. 2.

T: Excellent. When reading a paragraph, we should also pay attention to the relationship between paragraphs. Some sentences may tell us that.

【设计意图】 这一段落的处理方式与第一段不同。第一段是教师搭脚手架,引导学生去发现(discover)段落的结构和细节信息的组织方式。第二段撤脚手架,教师不再引导,学生自主操练(practise)分析段落结构的技能,对在第一段中发现的技能进行练习和巩固。在处理完段落结构的分析后,教师以问题形式引导学生深层阅读和思考,通过对第二段段首句的再次解读引导学生分析出第一段和第二段之间的逻辑关系。第二段的段首句不仅是该段的主题句还起着连接第一段、第二段的承上启下的作用。这一环节在原有基础上又带领学生上了一个新台阶,不仅关注段内细节信息的连接方式,还关注到段落之间的衔接。

Activity three: Read and apply — Para. 3 (6 mins)

Read Para. 3 and apply the skills they have learned to analyze the structure of Para. 3.

T: What are the details used to support the topic sentence? How are the details organized? Read and find out.

S21: (As the following chart shows)

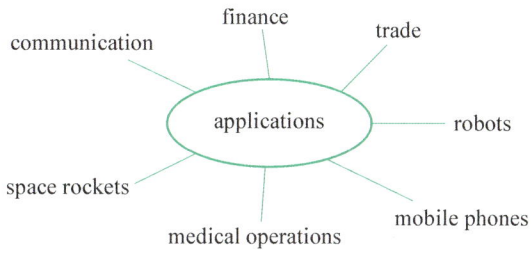

T: How are these details organized?

S21: The details are listed one by one.

T: Good. This is called "listing" (Note on blackboard). How are the details listed one by one?

S21: The linking words *and*, *also*, *as well as*, *even*.

T: Very good. "And, also, as well as, even" are used to list detailed information in this paragraph. What about the last two sentences? Are these two sentences the details to support the topic sentence?

S22: No. These two sentences serve as a conclusion.

T: Very good. So we should also pay attention and tell whether all the sentences are the details to support the topic sentence.

【设计意图】 这一步骤重在学生对所学技能的应用。三个环节对三个段落的处理方式不同。第一、二环节采用"归纳法",第三环节采用"演绎法"。在第一环节中,学生在教师的引导下分析第一段并归纳出段落结构和分析段落结构的方法。第二环节,在操练前面所学技能的基础上加以提升,归纳出分析句子之间、段落之间逻辑关系的分析方法。第二环节是对第一环节的巩固和提升。第一、二两个环节在阅读的过程中分析文本归纳出段落结构与衔接手段,即"归纳"。在第三环节中,应用和强化前面两个步骤所归纳的结论,即"演绎"。

Step 5: Thinking and discussing (5 mins)

Discuss in groups about the question: What's your attitude towards the influence of the development of computers on human beings? And then come up with supporting details.

S23: I think the development of the computer has a good effect on human beings. Because it connects people from all over the world and we can share information with others. The world is becoming smaller. It brings convenience to us.

S24: In my opinion, it also brings bad influence. With the development of computers, teenagers can watch violent videos and learn bad things from the Internet. They become addicted to computer games, which has a very bad effect on teenagers and their families.

Ss: ...

T: I'd like you to write down your opinion in a paragraph. First, state your opinion in the topic sentence. Then, give details to support your idea. Finally, organize your details naturally and logically using proper linking words.

【设计意图】 处理完课文信息后,让学生讨论如何看待计算机的发展对人类产生的影响。当今社会,计算机的快速发展在给人们带来便利的同时也带了一些负面的影响。通过此环节,让学生形成正确的价值观,批判地看待计算机快速发展这一现象。同时,要求学生用细节信息来支持自己的观点,为课后作业做准备。

2. 板书设计

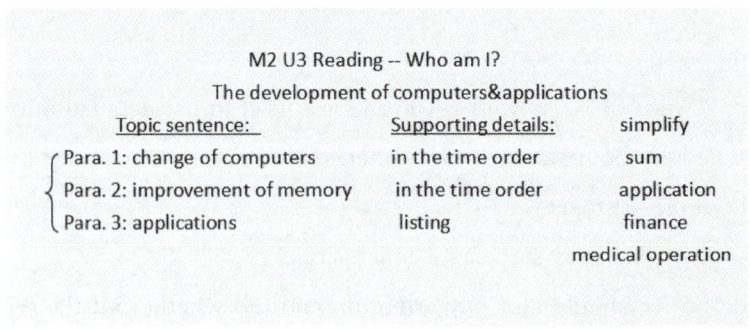

3. 作业布置

Write a paragraph about your attitude towards computers with a topic sentence and supporting details organized logically.

【设计意图】 让学生就"*the influence of the development of computers on human beings*"写一段话,用上主题句和支撑信息,并且合理地组织这些信息。让学生将文中所分析的段落结构学以致用,加以落实,合理地组织自己的观点。

(三) 教学反思

1. 多级任务驱动,解读段落结构

本堂课几个主要任务的设置层层递进,环环相扣。整个教学过程由任务驱动,任务的设置有梯度,通过教师搭脚手架、撤脚手架,先"归纳"再"演绎",从而实现教学目标。

分析段落结构和句子之间、段落之间的逻辑是重要的阅读技能,但是对现阶段的高一学生来说却是一个全新的挑战。再加上阅读文章的题材和专业术语都给学生的阅读增加了难度。因此,教师设置了多级任务,从易到难、从有教师引导到自主完成、从搭脚手架到撤脚手架、从"归纳"到"演绎"。在整个阅读过程中,学生在教师的引导下一步一步完成学习任务,一点一点掌握分析段落结构的方法。学生运用速读、跳读等阅读技能处理文章表层信息,准确理解文本大意。在教师脚手架的帮助下深入分析文本,归纳出段落结构和细节信息的组织方式。随着任务层层推进,在教师撤去脚手架后,能自主运用新技能在下一段语篇中进行演绎和应用,从而巩固和提高分析段落结构的能力,达到教学目标。

2. 分析篇章结构,训练逻辑思维

篇章是作者思维过程的体现,篇章的段落之间、句子之间都有其内在的逻辑关系。分析语篇结构、段落结构、句间关系是学生逻辑思维能力的体现,也是概要写作所需要的重要能力。逻辑思维能力是指对事物进行观察、比较、分析、综合、抽象、概括、判断、推理的能力。概要写作要求对文章进行高度概括和浓缩。要求学生具有准确理解篇章、区分主次、寻找关键词、概括段落大意、用自己的语言进行转述等能力。本堂课通过分析段落结构和各级任务的设置训练了学生区分主次、寻找关键词、确定主题句、判断句间关系等技能,强化了分析段落结构、归纳主旨大意、判断句子之间、段落之间的衔接等逻辑思维能力。

(教学设计撰写:温州第八高级中学 陈学丹)

教材文本

Unit 3 Computers
WHO AM I?

Over time I have been changed quite a lot. I began as a calculating machine in France in 1642. Although I was young I could simplify difficult sums. I developed very slowly and it took nearly two hundred years before I was built as an analytical machine by Charles Babbage. After I was programmed by an operator who used cards with holes, I could "think" logically and produce an answer quicker than any person. At that time it was considered a technological revolution and the start of my "artificial intelligence". In 1936 my real father, Alan Turing, wrote a book about how I could be made to work as a "universal machine" to solve any difficult mathematical problem. From then on, I grew rapidly both in size and in brainpower. By the 1940s I had grown as large as a room, and I wondered if I would grow any larger. However, this reality also worried my designers. As time went by, I was made smaller. First as a PC (personal computer) and then as a laptop, I have been used in offices and homes since the 1970s.

These changes only became possible as my memory improved. First it was stored in tubes, then on transistors and later on very small chips. As a result I totally changed my shape. As I have grown older I have also grown smaller. Over time my memory has developed so much that, like an elephant, I never forget anything I have been told! And my memory became so large that even I couldn't believe it! But I was always so lonely standing there by myself, until in the early 1960s they gave me a family connected by a network. I was able to share my knowledge with others through the World Wide Web.

Since the 1970s many new applications have been found for me. I have become very important in communication, finance and trade. I have also been put into robots and used to make mobile phones as well as help with medical operations. I have even been put into space rockets and sent to explore the Moon and Mars. Anyhow, my goal is to provide humans with a life of high quality. I am now truly filled with happiness that I am a devoted friend and helper of the human race!

 说课案例五（阅读课）

PEP NSEFC M5 U1 Great Scientists(Reading)

Good morning, ladies and gentlemen! I'm XX from XXXX. It's my great honor to be here to give a lesson plan presentation. The lesson I'm going to talk about is from Unit 1 *Great Scientists* in Module 5, NSEFC. The lesson type is Reading.

1. Analysis

The reading passage is about how John Snow defeats "King Cholera" by seven steps of doing a scientific research, namely find a problem, make a question, think of a method, collect information, analyze results, find supporting evidence and draw a conclusion. The students in my class have already known something about cholera like some symptoms through life experience and something about scientific researches through biology class, so their prior knowledge can reduce their comprehending difficulties. Besides, the passage uses some sentences of indirect description and contrast words to reflect John Snow's qualities. In this case, they may have trouble in interpreting these words and sentences in the text because of lacking certain methods of doing it. With the help of my scaffolds, involving seven steps of doing a scientific research and the guidance of interpretation, it won't be difficult for the students to comprehend different levels of reading questions and conclude John Snow's qualities through interpretation.

II. Statement

Based on analysis above, here come the learning objectives. First, by the end of the lesson, the students can locate detailed information about seven steps of doing the scientific research by scanning. Second, the students are able to retell the passage according to the key words provided on the blackboard. Third, the students will be able to work in groups to discuss John Snow's qualities through interpretation, which is also the learning focus and anticipated difficulty in this class.

III. Description

I will lead the students to achieve all those objectives and deal with the difficulty in the following teaching procedure.

The first teaching stage is pre-reading. In this part, I'll design a talking activity. I will ask the students whether they have once experienced some symptoms of cholera, which can activate their old knowledge store. Then the students are guided to ponder if someone is going to find out the cause of it, what he would do. By doing this, the seven steps of doing a scientific research will be presented. Thus, the basic structure of the passage is formed before reading and the students can make full preparations for reading comprehension.

In the while-reading stage, there are three steps. Step 1 is to read for comprehension. I'll follow seven steps of doing a scientific research for it's the basic framework of the passage. The students are going to read the passage for the first time and are given with display questions to locate and sort out key information in each step. In the step of finding a problem, the key information, "a deadly disease" is put forward; in making a question, "two theories with the latter one suspected" is discussed; in thinking of a method, "enquiry" is shared; in collecting information, "the map" is talked about; in analyzing results, "It seems water was to blame" is given; in finding supporting evidence, "two supporting evidence" is generalized; as for drawing a conclusion, "it proves water is to blame" is concluded. During the whole process, the students are also given the integration of referential questions and evaluative questions in the following steps. In the step of making a question, I will ask the students to tell the difference between two theories. The students are able to identify one is active while the other is passive. In the step of thinking of a method, the students are expected to evaluate the method "enquiry" by giving reasons. In the step of finding supporting evidence, the students are supposed to infer the pronoun "it" to fully understand the evidence John Snow found. With the purpose of letting the students have a clear picture about the whole passage, I will ask the students whether I can delete Para. 7, which is about the suggestion given by John Snow to develop their critical thinking. So the whole passage is comprehended based on the students' first reading under the framework of doing a scientific research, where different levels of questions are set to cultivate the students' thinking ability.

Step 2 is to read for interpretation. The students are going to read the whole passage for the second time and find out sentences and words that show the qualities of John Snow. Considering the students may encounter difficulties, I build scaffolds by setting three columns of interpretation. The first column is about interpreting sentences of indirect description, like "*This was a deadly disease of its day. Neither its cause nor its cure was understood.*" The students may come up with various words like *responsible* and *merciful* to describe John Snow. The second column is about interpreting contrast of noun phrases, like "*Queen Victoria & ordinary people*" and "*King cholera & poor neighborhood*". Through the contrast, the students may consider John Snow as a generous scientist who was concerned about ordinary people. The third column is about interpreting accurate verbs of the text in contrast to general verbs. By contrasting, the students may realize that John Snow held a serious attitude towards scientific research and was quite strict with himself. These three columns of interpretation are first done with the help of the teacher and then in group discussion and the last by individual work. This can help the students get used to self-study and group-study instead of listening to the teacher's instruction only.

Step 3 is to read for thinking. The students need to work in pairs to think about whether those adjectives from the last activity to describe John Snow are directly taken from the passage. They are going to identify the tone of the passage. Firstly, multiple choices are given to the students to judge whether the passage is objective or subjective. Then the students are going to read for the third time and find out more supporting evidence to prove the objectiveness of the passage, during which the students' logical thinking and critical thinking are involved.

In the while-reading stage, actually the three steps are closely related. Reading for comprehension is the basis of reading for interpretation, which is also the foundation for thinking. During the whole process, the students' thinking ability will be enhanced step by step.

The final stage is post-reading. And in this stage, I mainly focus on a retelling activity, which requires the students to retell the passage according to the key words on the blackboard. It can not only help the students consolidate what they've learned in class, but also serve as a reflection for teachers to check the students' learning performance.

Ⅳ. Exposition

In the end, the homework is assigned, that is, to develop the whole passage into a short paragraph around 80 words, aimed to check and reinforce what the students have learned in class.

Here is my blackboard design. The purpose is to show the learning focus and highlight the key information.

Ⅴ. Reflection

As to me, reading can not only provide a stage where students can improve their language competence, but also provide a platform to develop their thinking ability and shape their value. In this class, by reading the story of John Snow, the students are able to practise using scanning, inferring, summarizing and retelling skills to learn great deeds of this scientist. Meanwhile, they will get more familiar with seven steps of doing a scientific research and get influenced by John Snow's qualities. By doing so, their understanding of the whole passage will be deepened and their morality of life can be cultivated.

That's all about my lesson plan presentation. Thanks for attention.

（说课稿撰写：温州中学　夏一建）

 附：教学设计及教材文本

M5 U1 John Snow Defeats "King Cholera"

（一）教学分析

1. 教材分析

本课教材选自人教版《普通高中课程标准实验教科书英语必修5》第一单元,本单元的话

题是"伟大的科学家",主要围绕科学家的丰功伟绩和精神品质展开。阅读材料选自 Reading 部分,语篇主要以第三人称的视角讲述了科学家 John Snow 通过七个做科学实验的步骤找到了发生霍乱的根源。正文可分为七个部分,主要立足于发现问题、作出假设、明确方法、收集数据、分析数据、寻找证据和得出结论七个步骤层层深入,来挖掘 John Snow 作为一个伟大科学家在这过程中所体现的崇高的精神品质和科学严谨的实验态度。由于文章是说明文,且篇幅较长,因此学生需要立足于本文的框架,即七个步骤梳理文章的脉络,继而探索主人公的精神品质和科学素养。此外,文章中出现的生词较多,所以在进行深层次阅读之前要透彻理解文章的表层信息,并扫除文中的语言障碍。

本课的教学并不止停留在梳理 John Snow 的七个步骤和简单挖掘主人公的精神品质和科学素养,更是落脚在解读文章的遣词造句。通过解读文章的语言,不难发现作者巧妙的用词和构思都是为了凸显主人公的精神品质和科学素养。因此,学生需要在揣摩原文词句的基础上,体会字里行间所表达的情感,感受主人公 John Snow 伟大的人格魅力,这也是文章的亮点和难点所在。

2. 学生分析

本班学生来自某重点中学的高二年级,他们通过前三个学期的学习已经初步达到《普通高中英语课程标准》所规定的六级能力,即能够独立进行较为流畅的语言表达,能够通过上下文理解生词,能够推测代词的指代,以及根据关键词来复述整篇课文等。此外,他们通过自己的生活经验和生物课所学知识,已经了解了一些与霍乱相关的知识和做科学实验的基本步骤,所以他们的背景知识在一定程度上能降低学习难度。但是,虽有良好的英语学习基础,学生的思维能力仍有待提高,学生对于文章遣词造句的解读缺乏一定的敏感度,还不能做到独立解读文章的语言,且缺少方法的指导。总之,本班大部分学生英语基础相对较扎实,语言的产出能力较强,但是在深层思维参与的活动如语言的解读方面存在一定的困难。

本班多数学生性格较为活泼,喜欢合作和讨论来完成学习任务,课堂的参与度较高,但不易在课堂上沉下心来钻研思考。因此,课堂上设置一些小组讨论、同桌合作等任务来激发学生的学习兴趣,同时也将展开一系列不同层次的提问来提高学生独立思考的能力。

3. 教学目标

1)语言能力与学习能力

(1)通过寻读快速定位与 John Snow 和七个科学实验步骤有关的细节信息;

(2)根据板书上提炼出的七个步骤的关键词对文章进行复述,运用文本中所学的关于科学实验步骤的相关词汇,如 theory, suspect 等;

(3)积极地参与话题为 John Snow 伟大精神品质和科学态度的小组讨论。

2)文化意识与思维品质

(1)解读文章遣词造句背后所体现的 John Snow 的精神品质和科学态度;

(2)辩证地判定最后一段与科学实验步骤相关与否及其作用。

4. 教学重难点

本课教学重点为理清做科学实验的七个步骤,并通过文章的遣词造句来探索主人公 John Snow 的精神品质和科学素养。教学活动主要聚焦发现霍乱病原的七个实验步骤,并在这个框架内处理文章的基本信息,并通过一些侧面描写的句子、蕴含对比含义的名词短语和精准动词等解读来探究 John Snow 的人格魅力。本节课的难点主要是基于学生的思维能力,透过文章的用词看到背后所要传达的情感含义。

5. 教学思路

本课课型为阅读课,根据教学计划划分为三个阶段,即读前、读中和读后。读前激活学生背景知识,建构阅读框架;读中梳理文章脉络,立足文章主线展开分析;读后放眼学生基于全文的产出,进行文章复述。本节课共包括 5 个活动。活动一为读前调查访谈,教师询问学生是否有经历过霍乱的一些症状来唤醒学生的已有知识,为读中阶段做好铺垫;活动二为读中对文章内容的理解,教师引导学生理清做科学实验的七个步骤,通过寻读抓出关于这七个步骤的基本信息和提炼每个步骤中的关键词;活动三为读中对文章语言的解读,教师引导学生抓出文章中侧面描写的句子、蕴含对比含义的名词短语以及精准动词,并通过对它们的解读来探究 John Snow 的精神品质和科学素养;活动四为读中对行文基调的思考,教师通过启发学生思考文中是否直接评述了 John Snow 的精神品质和科学素养,关注行文是如何客观地记叙了该伟大的科学家;活动五为读后复述,教师重述本堂课的教学重点,引导学生利用板书上关于七个步骤以及 John Snow 精神品质和科学素养方面的关键词对文章进行复述,并提出课后将其写成 80 字左右小短文的要求。

(二) 教学过程

1. 教学活动

Step 1: Pre-reading (3 mins)

Activity. Free talk (3 mins)

Talk about whether students have once experienced some symptoms of cholera, like stomachache, dry skin, vomit. After that, they are required to talk about steps of doing scientific researches according to what they have learned in biology class.

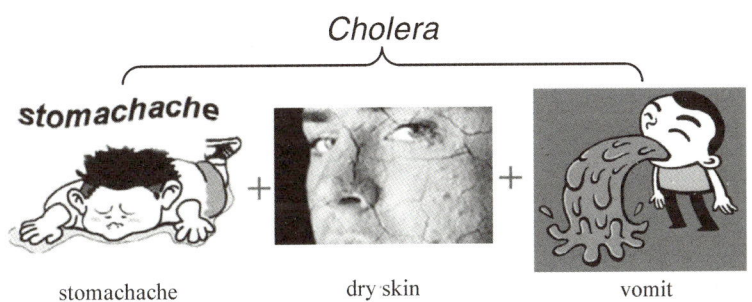

T: First of all, let's do a survey. Have you ever experienced stomachache, dry skin, or vomit?

Ss: Yes/No. (T invites one of them to share the experience of his or her suffering.)

T: If you have these symptoms happening together, what would you get?

Ss: Cholera.

T: Exactly, you are likely to get cholera. In British history, the cholera broke out. People were so terrified at that time but they didn't know the cause. In order to find it out, what should they do?

Ss: If they have found that the problem is cholera, then they should make a question, think of a method, collect information, analyze results, find supporting evidence and make a conclusion.

T: It seems that you are doing quite well in biology. When we are going to do a scientific research, first, we should find a problem. Then we are going to make a question, think of a method, collect information, analyze results, find supporting evidence and draw a conclusion, which actually is how this passage is organized.

【设计意图】 调查和询问与文章内容相关的知识能够激活学生的背景图式。在这个活动中,通过调查学生是否经历过霍乱的一些症状,使学生建构有关霍乱的概念,激发学生的学习兴趣。同时,在读前为学生搭建整篇文章的框架,即做实验的七个步骤,为阅读搭建结构支架。

Step 2: While-reading (32 mins)

Activity 1. Read for comprehension (17 mins)

Read the passage for the first time to comprehend seven steps of doing scientific research (in this text, specifically finding the cause of the cholera). They are supposed to locate and sort out key information of each step to lay a solid foundation for retelling.

Finding a problem (Para. 1)

Read Paragraph 1, answer the following questions and share feelings after reading.

Q1: What was the problem?

Q2: Why was it called "king cholera" as the title suggests?

T: In Paragraph 1, which step of doing scientific research is mentioned?

S1: Find a problem.

T: What was the problem?

S1: Cholera.

T: Very Good. You give me the key word "cholera". However, as the title suggests, it was called King Cholera, not simply cholera. Why?

S2: This was a deadly disease of its day. /So many people died every time there was an outbreak.

T: Exactly. What's your feeling after reading these sentences?

S2: I feel horrible/terrible/scared…

Making a question & think of a method (Para. 2 – 3)

Read Paragraph 2 and 3 to find the theories John Snow believed in as well as tell the difference between two theories. Then, they are asked to identify his method with evaluation.

Q1: What theory did John Snow believe in? What's the difference of theories mentioned in the text?

Q2: Which method did John Snow apply? What do you think of it?

T: After finding the problem, cholera, what did John Snow do next?

Ss: Make a question.

T: In order to make a question, John Snow should refer to some theories. How many theories were mentioned?

Ss: 2.

T: What are they? /What's the difference between them? /Which one did he believe in? /Was he sure enough?

S3 & 4: One is that cholera multiplied in the air, and the other is that people absorbed it with meals. The former is passive while the latter active. He believed the latter. He was not sure enough, because he suspected it.

T: In order to make sure of it, what kind of method did he apply? Find out a word in the text.

S5: Enquiry.

T: Exactly! What do you think of this method and why?

S5: Useful, effective… because…

Collecting information & analyze results (Para. 4)

Read Paragraph 4 to find out his way of collecting information and his findings. Then they are led to conclude the results and John Snow's attitude towards it.

Q1: How did he collect information?

Q2: And what did he find?

Q3: What result did he conclude?

Q4: Was he sure enough at this time?

T: After reading Paragraph 4, what's his way of collecting information?

Ss: By using a map.

T: Excellent. Now observe the map and tell me what happened to these areas in circle and in rhombus?

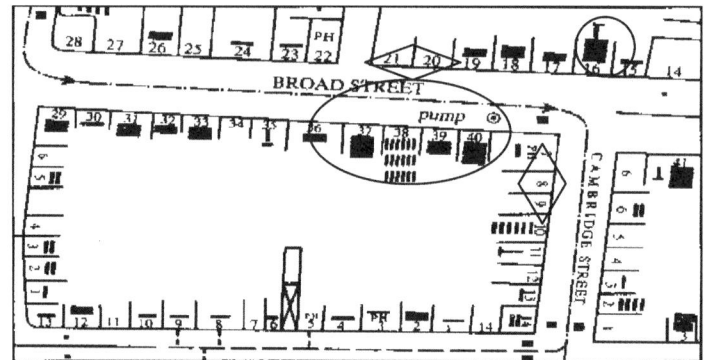

Note: ⋯ : 1 death PH: public house 30,31,…: numbers of houses

S6: Many deaths/no deaths.

T: Why? What caused the difference?

S6: Whether they drank water from the pump.

T: Perfect. That's what John Snow found. By the way, do you think John Snow could solve this problem without the map? Give your reasons.

S7: I don't think so, because the map gave him exact and valuable clues.

T: Next, based on the map, what conclusion did he draw?

S8: The water was to blame.

T: You said the water was to blame, does that mean John Snow was sure enough?

S8: Not sure, because it seemed that the water was to blame.

Finding supporting evidence & draw a conclusion (Para. 5-6)

Read Paragraph 5-6 to sort out the evidence John Snow found and think about John Snow's attitude towards whether he was sure enough about the evidence.

Q1: What evidence did John Snow find? Was he sure enough about it?

Q2: What's the other evidence he found?

Q3: Was he sure enough this time? Why?

T: What evidence did John Snow find at first?

Ss: He found that it came from the river polluted by the dirty water from London.

T: Yes, what does "it" refer to? Which one?

> Sentence: He found that it came from the river polluted by the dirty water from London.
> What does "it" refer to?
> A. cholera;   B. water supplied for two streets;   C. the dirty water from London
> Key: B

Ss: B.

T: Exactly. But do you think it's enough to prove the cause of cholera?

Ss: Not enough, because of the limited number of evidence.

T: How about John Snow? Did he think it's enough?

Ss: Not enough.

T: Yes, so he needed more evidence. What's the other evidence he found?

S9: He found a woman and her daughter died of cholera after drinking the water from the pump as well.

T: Quite right, so was he sure enough this time?

Ss: He was quite sure this time.

T: Brilliant. That's why he drew the conclusion that polluted water carried germs with certainty.

Giving a suggestion (Para. 7)

Think about whether the last paragraph can be deleted or not. If not, they are supposed to analyze the function of it.

Q1: Can Paragraph 7 be deleted?

Q2: What does Paragraph 7 tell us?

T: Now that the conclusion has been made and all the steps of doing scientific research have been finished, so can Paragraph 7 be deleted?

Ss: No.

T: What does Paragraph 7 tell us?

S10: After making a conclusion of the research, John Snow made a suggestion so that the illness could be prevented.

【设计意图】 该部分为读中理解。通过建构文章的框架,即做科学实验的七个步骤,为学生理清文章的脉络。在这个框架中,学生需要对各个步骤中的相关信息进行处理,比如John Snow 所感兴趣的两个理论的区别,John Snow 所使用的方法并对之做出评价,以及通过上下文的指代关系推测代词的含义等。每个步骤都由不同层次的设问构成,包括展示性问题和参考性问题。本部分教师的主要关注点在于学生对文章基本信息的处理和文章主线的提取,并将关键信息以板书的方式加以呈现。因此,为把握好这一重点,应给予学生充足的阅读时间,使他们在全面理解文章的基础上建立文章的框架,为接下来的语言解读活动夯实基础。

Activity 2. Read for interpretation (10 mins)

Read the passage for the second time to interpret the language of the text within three columns, including sentences of indirect description, contrast of noun phrases and accurate verbs to show the qualities of John Snow. The first column is about interpreting sentences of indirect description. They are going to finish it with the help of the teacher and the next noun phrases interpretation in a group discussion and the last verbs interpretation by individual work.

Column 1 (sentences of indirect description):

This was a deadly disease of its day. Neither its cause nor its cure was understood. So many terrified people died every time there was an outbreak.

From the stomach the disease quickly attacked the body and soon the affected person died.

...

Insights: **To emphasize John Snow was responsible and merciful from an indirect description.**

T: Through seven steps of finding the cause of cholera, we are aware of the great qualities of John Snow. Now it's your time to use some adjectives to describe him and find out the corresponding sentences of indirect description to support your ideas.

S11: I think he was responsible/caring/thoughtful/..., because ...

S12: ...

Column 2 (contrast of noun phrases):

Pair 1: Queen Victoria & ordinary people

Pair 2: King cholera & poor neighborhood

...

Insights: **John Snow was generous and concerned about ordinary people.**

T: Now can you find out any contrast of some noun phrases that reflect John Snow' qualities?

S13: Queen Victoria and ordinary people; King cholera and poor neighborhood.

T: You are very quick-minded. So what kind of words will you use to describe John Snow?

S13: He was generous/caring/quick-minded/...

Column 3 (accurate verbs)	
John Snow <u>suspected</u> that the second theory ... First he <u>marked</u> on a map the exact places ... He also <u>noticed</u> that houses ... He <u>discovered</u> that these people worked in the pub ...	John Snow believed that the second theory ... First he wrote the exact places ... He also saw that houses ... He found that these people worked in the pub ...
Insights: **The accurate verbs show John Snow held a serious attitude towards the scientific research and was quite strict with himself.**	

T: What kind of verbs can you find that vividly show John Snow's qualities?

Ss: Suspect, mark ...

T: Good job! Now let's contrast the left with the right one. Through the contrast, what do you think of John Snow from these verbs?

S14: He was quite serious about the research and he was hard-working and careful.

【设计意图】 虽然前一个活动对文章的基本信息处理得较为透彻,但是上升到对语言的深度分析,难度仍然较大。针对本堂课的教学难点,教师根据学生学情,将语言的解读分成三个部分,分别是侧面描写的句子解读、蕴含对比含义的名词短语解读以及准确动词的比较解读。无疑,在这三个维度下,教学指向明确,有利于学生分析和提炼语言。本环节设计不仅仅停留在语言的解读,更是探索和挖掘John Snow伟大的精神品质和严谨的科学态度。

Activity 3. Read for thinking (5 mins)

Work in pairs to think about whether those adjectives are directly taken from the passage and identify the tone of the passage.

Do you find these adjectives directly from the text?

What's the tone of the passage?

A. Objective.   B. Subjective.

Other ways to show the objectiveness of the passage: third-person point of view; numbers

---

T: Now let's have a further thinking, do you find these adjectives directly from the text?

Ss: No.

T: So what's the tone of this passage?

Ss: A.

T: Quite right. Any other ways to show this tone?

S15: The whole passage is written from the third point of view and adopts many numbers to show the objectiveness.

【设计意图】 该活动与前一活动的语言解读相辅相成:解读文章的语言激活了学生的思维,同时也为判断文章的行文基调做好铺垫。在语言解读活动中,学生对于 John Snow 伟大的精神品质和严谨的科学态度的描述,主要是来源于对文章信息的加工与概括,这恰恰说明了文章的客观性。然后基于文章的客观性,学生需要去寻找其它能够佐证这一说法的依据。在这个过程中,学生的逻辑思维能力和批判性思维能力得到了潜移默化的提高。

Step 3: Post-reading (5 mins)

Activity. Read for retelling (5 mins)

Retell the story according to key words provided on the blackboard.

T: Now look at the key words on the blackboard and retell the passage.

S16 - 18: ...

【设计意图】 读后复述,巩固课堂所学。教师通过板书来重述本堂课重点,即做科学研究的七个步骤及 John Snow 伟大的精神品质和严谨的科学态度。学生需要根据板书上所提炼出的关键词对文章进行简要的概括复述。复述有利于教师检测学生整堂课的学习情况,也有助于学生的自我检测与反思。

2. 板书设计

	John Snow Defeats "King Cholera"	
find a problem	a deadly disease	qualities
make a question	2 theories (2nd suspected)	responsible
think of a method	enquiry	merciful
collect information	mark on the map	generous
analyze results	water (seem)	strict
find supporting evidence	x2	serious attitude
draw a conclusion	water (prove)	……
make a suggestion		

3. 作业布置

Develop your retelling into a short passage about 60 - 80 words.

(三)教学反思

对于一堂阅读课而言,在有限的时间内实现面面俱到不太可能,所以筛选教学内容,突出教学的重点成为教学设计的关键所在。随着英语学科核心素养的推行,英语课堂不仅仅停留在训练和提升学生的语言技能,还强调关注学生思维的发展和文化意识的提升,这赋予了英语教学新的生命。

1. 筛选教学内容,突出教学重点

筛选教学内容的前提是教学重点的确定。以本课教学设计为例,笔者从多维度解读文本,突出文本的两条主线,即教学的重点:明线为做科学实验的七个步骤,暗线为通过文章的遣词造句来挖掘和探索主人公 John Snow 伟大的精神品质和严谨的科学态度。本节课对于明线的处理贯穿了整个教学设计。读前通过情境导入,使学生建构了文章的行文框架,即做科学实验的七个步骤。读中的文章内容理解也是根据这七个步骤,然后对每一个步骤中的关键信息进行提取与加工。读后的文章复述同样是基于科学实验的七个步骤,对课堂所学进行了巩固。本节课对于暗线的处理则建立在明线疏通文章内容的基础之上,然后去定位侧面描写的句子、蕴含对比含义的名词短语以及精准动词,通过解读和比较,来总结概括 John Snow 的精神品质和科学态度。所以本堂课的教学紧紧围绕教学重点来对教学内容进行筛选,实现重点知识的复现,让学生"学精",从而真正落实课堂所学。

2. 关注思维教学,品读人文精神

阅读并不仅仅是为了读懂文章的大意,或是文章的表层信息,还在于思维能力的发展和文化品格的熏陶。一方面,本节课学生通过学习 John Snow 发现霍乱根源的伟大事迹,操练了寻读、推断、总结和复述等语言技能;另一方面,学生通过文章内容理解、文章语言解读、行文基调思考三个部分提升了思维能力。内容理解是为了更好地解读语言,解读语言为思考行文基调铺平道路。在这个过程中,学生的思维能力逐步提升,是一个循序渐进的过程,这有赖于读中不同层次的问题设置,比如展示性问题、参阅性问题和评价性问题的有机结合。与此同时,文章的语言解读旨在引导学生根据要求定位相应词句,来体会主人公 John Snow 伟大的精神品质和严谨的科学态度,进而潜移默化地影响和塑造学生的价值观。所以这节课的教学目标并不仅仅停留在提高学生的语言技能,还关注学生的思维发展和人文精神的熏陶。

(教学设计撰写:温州中学 夏一建)

教材文本

JOHN SNOW DEFEATS "KING CHOLERA"

John Snow was a famous doctor in London — so expert, indeed, that he attended Queen Victoria as her personal physician. But he became inspired when he thought about helping ordinary people exposed to cholera. This was the deadly disease of its day. Neither its cause nor its cure was understood. So many thousands of terrified people died every time there was an outbreak. John Snow wanted to face the challenge and solve this problem. He knew that cholera would never be controlled until its cause was found.

He became interested in two theories that possibly explained how cholera killed people. The first suggested that cholera multiplied in the air. A cloud of dangerous gas floated around until it found its victims. The second suggested that people absorbed this disease into their bodies with their meals. From the stomach the disease quickly attacked the body and soon the affected person died.

John Snow suspected that the second theory was correct but he needed evidence. So when another outbreak hit London in 1854, he was ready to begin his enquiry. As the disease spread quickly through poor neighborhoods, he began to gather information. In two particular streets, the cholera outbreak was so severe that more than 500 people died in ten days. He was determined to find out why.

First, he marked on a map the exact places where all the dead people had lived. This gave him a valuable clue about the cause of the disease. Many of the deaths were near the water pump in Broad Street (especially numbers 16, 37, 38 and 40). He also noticed that some houses (such as 20 and 21 Broad Street and 8 and 9 Cambridge Street) had had no deaths. He had not foreseen this, so he made further investigations. He discovered that these people worked in the pub at 7 Cambridge Street. They had been given free beer and so had not drunk the water from the pump. It seemed that the water was to blame.

Next, John Snow looked into the source of the water for these two streets. He found that it came from the river polluted by the dirty water from London. He immediately told the astonished people in Broad Street to remove the handle from the pump so that it could not be used. Soon afterwards the disease slowed down. He had shown that cholera was spread by germs and not in a cloud of gas.

In another part of London, he found supporting evidence from two other deaths that were linked to the Broad Street outbreak. A woman, who had moved away from Broad Street, liked the water from the pump so much that she had it delivered to her house every day. Both she and her daughter died of cholera after drinking the water. With this extra evidence John Snow was able to announce with certainty that polluted water carried the virus.

To prevent this from happening again, John Snow suggested that the source of all the water supplies be examined. The water companies were instructed not to expose people to polluted water any more. Finally "King Cholera" was defeated.

PEP NSEFC M4 U3 A Master of Nonverbal Humor (Reading)

Good afternoon, everyone! I'm XX from XXXX. It's my great honor to present my lesson plan. The lesson I'm going to talk about is from Unit 3 *A Master of Nonverbal Humor* in Module 4. The lesson type is reading.

I. Analysis

The passage mainly talks about the famous actor Charlie Chaplin. There are five paragraphs in this passage, introducing respectively Chaplin's popularity, his childhood and his teenager life, his famous image "the Little Tramp", a scene in *The Gold Rush*, Chaplin's achievements and people's love towards him. These are actually the five elements that lead to his success as a master. Thus, the five elements become the outline of the text and the word *Master* the clue of reading the passage as well as the key to the understanding of Chaplin. As inferring and summarizing are two not well-developed skills for the students, they will have difficulty in extracting the five elements leading to Chaplin's being a master. Thus, the teacher is supposed to provide scaffolding to make the reading process easy and smooth. Besides, the language in this passage is vivid and of moderate difficulty, which provides good examples for the students to learn, appreciate and apply. The two figures of speech in the text, litotes and simile, though familiar to the students, can make it hard for the students to appreciate the success and good qualities of Chaplin. Thus, more examples and explanations will be given as a support for the students' better understanding.

II. Statement

According to the analysis above, here come the learning objectives. First, by the end of the class, the students will be able to use skimming and scanning to find out some basic information about Chaplin. Second, the students are required to use the reading skills of inferring and summarizing to conclude five elements of Chaplin's success, and deepen the understanding of the title. As it is the learning focus as well as the difficult point of this class, the students will conclude the five elements in the careful reading activity. In order to lower the difficulty of summarizing, I have designed questions of both lower-order thinking ability and higher-order thinking ability to provide scaffolding. Third, the students will learn two figures of speech, litotes and simile in the text. Since this is another difficult point in this lesson, I will analyze them by giving examples and then ask students to make sentences. In this way, the students will have a better understanding of Chaplin.

III. Description

According to Bloom's Taxonomy, learning can be divided into six levels, namely, knowledge, comprehension, application, analysis, synthesis and evaluation. The former three levels belong to the lower-order thinking ability, and the latter three levels belong to the higher-order thinking ability. With the purpose of developing students' higher-order thinking ability as well as achieving all the learning objectives in this lesson, two kinds of questions are involved — questions of lower-order thinking ability and questions of higher-order thinking ability. Both kinds of questions are adopted throughout the teaching procedures. In the pre-reading stage, questions of lower-order thinking ability are designed to arouse students' interest and form a general concept of Chaplin. In the while-reading stage, questions of lower-order thinking ability are used to offer detailed information about Chaplin, which helps the students to understand the passage better. Then, questions of higher-order thinking ability are given with the purpose of summarizing the five elements of Chaplin's becoming a master and appreciating his excellent performance. In the post-reading stage, questions of higher-order thinking ability are designed to help them further comprehend the word "master". With the analysis above, I will explain each stage in detail.

Stage 1 Pre-reading

In the pre-reading stage, there are two activities. First of all, I'll show the video of *The Little Bread Dance* in the movie *The Gold Rush*, and ask two questions: What do you think of the video? What do you think of the character and his performance? This activity can arose the students' interest and lead to the topic. The second activity is brainstorming. I will ask my students to say something about Charlie Chaplin as much as possible. They are required to find out who Chaplin is and think about what qualities make him a master. It aims to activate their existing schema, and form a general concept of Chaplin, which lays the foundation for the later activities.

Stage 2 While-reading

Then, in the second stage, while-reading, I will ask the students to read the passage quickly and find out the information about Chaplin, and match the main idea of each paragraph. This activity can help drill students' reading skills of skimming and scanning. After getting the basic information about Chaplin, the students can have a better understanding of the text. Next, I will guide the students to read the passage paragraph by paragraph with the purpose of getting five major elements to explain the reason why Chaplin is called "A Master of Nonverbal Humor". Now I will introduce the five paragraphs respectively.

In the first paragraph, three questions will be asked: 1. What was the life background of people living at that time? How did they feel? 2. Why do you think Chaplin was popular at that time? 3. What is the element leading to Chaplin's mastery of acting? As is mentioned before, concluding the five elements for Chaplin to become a master is the learning focus as well as the difficult point in this class. In order to lower the difficulty of inferring and summarizing the elements, firstly, I will ask two questions of lower-order thinking ability to provide students with the historical background and people's attitudes towards Chaplin, thus enabling students to analyze why Chaplin was popular. This offers the clue for the next question. Then, from the third question which requires high-order thinking ability, the students will be able to conclude that one element that leads to Chaplin's master of acting is to make contribution to the society. This paragraph provides sample for the students to analyze the following questions, that is, to get the basic information first, and then conclude the element to be a master.

In the second paragraph, I will first explain the words "astonishing" and "worse off", then ask the following questions: 1. Was Chaplin's own life easy? Can you find some supporting details? 2. Based on the details, what is the second element that makes Chaplin a master? As we know, developing the higher-order thinking ability is a process of recurring, which means the students need some scaffolds to develop their thinking ability little by little. Therefore, for the first question, I design a question to offer the students some information about Chaplin's childhood experience, and let them understand the difficulties he met with during the childhood. Based on the detailed information, students can answer the second question and conclude that one element to become a master is to have good qualities such as being strong-minded, optimistic and caring. Then I will introduce the figure of speech — litotes. In this part, the students are required to find out some sentences according to my example, and I will explain its usage to help students gain a better understanding of Chaplin's valuable qualities, thus letting them fully perceive Chaplin as a master.

When it comes to the third paragraph, the students are supposed to find out details about Chaplin's famous image, and then answer the following questions: 1. What did he dress himself in? What was unusual about his outfit? 2. Why did he dress up like this? 3. Why did people like him? 4. What element can you infer to be a master from this paragraph? This paragraph aims to develop a specific kind of higher-order thinking ability, that is, critical thinking ability. It requires students to read between lines. With this purpose, I will guide them to find out little tramp's typical dress, then ask them to analyze the reason why he dressed up like this, the reason why people liked him and his personalities. These questions require the students to infer reasons based on their background information, which will be helpful to develop their critical thinking ability. At the same time, from the typical image that Chaplin created, the students can conclude that one element to become a master is to find a way that suits him best.

Next, in the fourth paragraph, after finding out the basic information about the movie *The Gold Rush*, I will guide the students to understand the figure of speech — simile. To cope with the difficulty of learning simile, I will first analyze two sentences in the passage, and then ask them to make sentences according to the picture. This activity can let the students be familiar with the figure of speech, thus help them understand Chaplin better. Besides, I will ask them to underline the verbs in this paragraph, make a conversation with the verbs and act it out. After the acting, I will ask questions to help the students have a further thinking about Chaplin and his performance. These activities will not only arouse their enthusiasm, but also help them appreciate Chaplin's excellent performance and then understand the reason why he is called "master", thus drawing the conclusion that having a good command of skills contributes to his becoming a master.

Lastly, I will center on the fifth paragraph by asking three questions: 1. What award did Chaplin win? 2. What was Chaplin besides an actor? 3. What's the element to be a master according to this paragraph? In the paragraph, two questions of lower-order thinking ability are given to get the information about Chaplin, and then students are required to summarize the last element to become a master — to get achievements in his career. So far, the students have already concluded Chaplin's five elements to become a master.

Up to now, the whole passage is analyzed in detail in order to let students understand the gist of the passage. Then, it comes to the final stage.

The final stage is post-reading, and in this stage, I mainly focus on helping students consolidate what they've learned in class and further developing their higher-order thinking ability. In the activities above, goals are set to help them conclude the five elements, and on the basis of the information, students already had enough language knowledge to explain their understanding of the title. In addition, with the enlightenment of five elements for Chaplin to become a master, the students will have a discussion to make their own elements to become a master. By carrying out these activities, students are expected to form their own understanding of the word "master".

Ⅳ. Exposition

Now comes the homework. The homework is to watch *The Little Bread Dance* again, and describe Chaplin's actions in detail as the author did in Paragraph 4. Then, the students are required to use the figures of speech they've learned today to write a passage in about 80 words. I design this homework in order to let students practice the figures of speech to fully understand the little tramp's glamour.

Here is my blackboard design. It highlights the teaching clues and increases the teaching efficiency.

Ⅴ. Reflection

To sum up, reading is not only a tool to improve students' abilities to use the language, but also a platform where students can discover the beauty of human nature while learning the language. In this lesson, all the activities follow the clue of how to become a master. The students are led to understand the elements that make Chaplin a master, and thus at the end of the class, they can have the affects and language to design their own elements of being a master. In short, this lesson has a very clear focus.

That's all for my lesson plan presentation. Thanks for your attention.

（说课稿撰写：浙江大学附属中学　倪晗）

附：教学设计及教材文本

M4 U3 A Master of Nonverbal Humor

（一）教学分析

1. 教材分析

本课教材选自人教版《普通高中课程标准实验教科书英语必修4》第三单元 Reading 部分。该文章主要讲述了著名幽默大师 Chaplin 的故事。作者透过文章标题说明了 Chaplin 的一生及其成就，并传达了人们对他的敬仰与喜爱。本文分为五段，分别讲述了 Chaplin 的风靡程度，他青少年时期的生活，他塑造的形象"小流浪汉"，他在电影 *The Gold Rush* 中的精彩片段以及人们对他的喜爱。以 master 一词为着力点，作者从为社会做出贡献、在某领域有所成就、找到适合自身的方法、拥有良好的技能以及拥有乐观、坚韧不拔、关心他人等良好品质这五个要素对 Chaplin 进行了详细说明。这五个要素不仅是文本的写作脉络，也是教学的推进线索,更是人物评价的基础。本文语言生动,难易适中,但是,文本中出现了比喻和反叙的修辞手法,需要教师的解释引导,从而让学生更好地解读文本,理解 Chaplin 被称为"大师"的原因。

2. 学生分析

本节课的学生来自浙江某高中高二年级。他们已经掌握了略读与找读的阅读技能,能够快速地从文中找出关于 Chaplin 的基本信息;已拥有一定的概括能力,但还不能独立处理高层次的问题,需要教师搭建支架进行帮助。该班级学生性格外向,敢于表达自己观点,为课堂活动顺利展开奠定了良好的基础。但是,学生个体英语能力有所差异,尤其是英语基础较薄弱的学生,需要教师通过图片展示或表格呈现等方式降低任务难度,并设计一些难度较低的问题来鼓励他们参与到课堂之中,提高英语学习的热情。

3. 教学目标

1) 语言能力

学生能够理解反叙、比喻等修辞格在文中的作用,并能够学以致用;能够运用找读和略读的阅读技巧,找到关于 Chaplin 和 *Gold Rush* 的关键信息;能够分析文章内容,通过概括、判断和推测等阅读技巧概括 Chaplin 成为大师的五要素;学生能够读懂文章的主旨和作者的写作意图,并明白 master 一词在文本中的具体含义。

2) 思维品质

学生能够运用推测、概括、归纳等技巧归纳卓别林成为大师的五要素,并对标题进行深入理解,从而发展学生的批判性思维能力。

3) 文化意识

学生能对《淘金记》的背景有所了解,并对美国淘金热的历史有更深体会;通过分析 Chaplin 成为大师的五要素,对外国幽默大师的优秀品质进行了解与学习。

4) 学习能力

(1) 学生能够运用认知策略,通过推测、概括等技巧来分析并解决问题。例如,他们能够分析小流浪汉的衣着背后的原因;能够借助图片、视频和其它非言语信息加深对 Chaplin 的整体感知。

(2) 学生能够运用交际策略,积极与同学交流,通过解释、重复、举例等方式表达自身想法。在读后活动中,小组讨论的形式能够加强他们的合作意识。此外,以文本对 Chaplin 的描写为依据,撰写对话并进行表演的读中活动要求学生互相交流想法,整合组员的观点,最终完成对话,有利于促进学生的交际能力。

4. 教学重难点

(1) 教学重点

本课的教学重点为总结 Chaplin 成为大师的五要素。通过概括文章每一段的段落大意,分析 Chaplin 被称作"非语言幽默大师"的原因等主要的教学活动,完成对其成为大师的五要素的总结。此外,本课还会侧重锻炼学生学习使用文章中丰富的语言来描述人物外貌和性格,例如 walk around stiffly,pick out,chewing 等,从而积累语言知识。

(2) 教学难点

文本中出现的修辞手法会是文章的难点之一。在文章中,修辞手法的频繁出现无疑增加了文章难度。此外,概括 Chaplin 的品质是本课的另一难点,该活动对学生的概括能力提出了更高的要求。

5. 教学思路

本课采取了自上而下的 PWP 交际教学模式。整节课由读前、读中和读后三部分构成。依据布鲁姆(Bloom)的教育目标分类学,思维过程可以具体化为知识、领会、应用、分析、综合和评价六个不同层次,而塔纳尔(Taner)对此进行了进一步的层次划分,将知识、领会和应用归为低阶思维能力,而分析、综合和评价归为高阶思维能力。笔者将高阶思维能力和低阶思维能力的问题进行整合,贯穿于整个课堂。在读前阶段,笔者会运用视频导入,利用低层次思维能力问题激活学生的已有图式和背景知识。在读中阶段,笔者将把低阶思维能力问题和高阶思维能力问题相结合,从而发展学生的思维能力。教师会运用图片和表格分析文本,引导学生逐一概括每一段的段落大意,最终得出卓别林成为大师的五要素。同时,教师会引导学生对文章中的修辞手法进行赏析。在读后阶段,笔者设计了两个高阶思维能力的问题,先让学生对标题进行深度解读,再让学生展开小组讨论,思考自身的成功之路。具体流程见图 1。

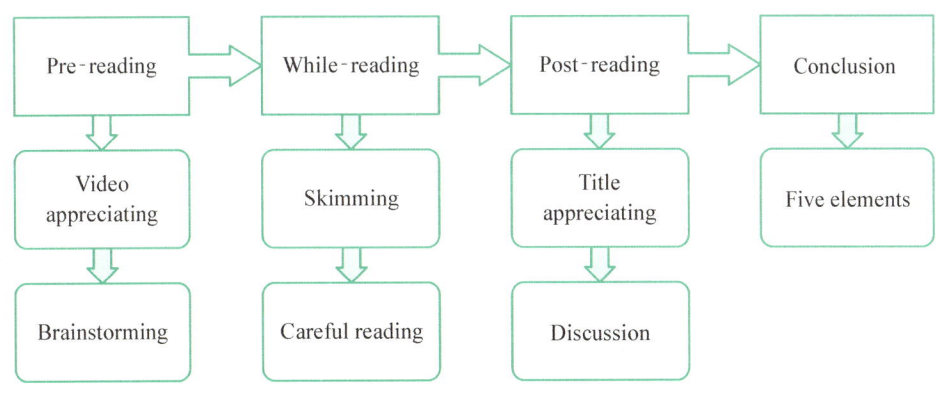

图 1　教学思路设计图

(二) 教学过程

1. 教学活动

Step 1: Pre-reading (4 mins)

Activity 1. Video appreciating (2 mins)

Watch the video *The Little Bread Dance* in the movie *The Gold Rush*, and answer the questions:

Q1: What do you think of the video?

Q2: What do you think of the character and his performance?

T: Watch this short video, and think about two questions: What do you think of the video? What do you think of the character's performance?

Ss: ...

T: What do you think of the video?

S1: It's funny and interesting.

T: What's the character's name?

S2: Charlie Chaplin.

T: Yes, Charlie Chaplin. What do you think about his performance?

S3: It is wonderful. /I can't fully understand his performance.

【设计说明】 运用一段来自《淘金记》的片段小面包舞来吸引学生,快速导入话题,从而引出本文人物 Chaplin。此外,该视频也为头脑风暴做下铺垫。

Activity 2. Brainstorming (2 mins)

Say something about Charlie Chaplin as much as possible and analyze the meaning of "master" and "nonverbal humor" in the title. Then find out who Chaplin is and think about what qualities make him a master.

T: Do you know much about Charlie Chaplin? According to the video, the title and the picture on the textbook, can you say something about him?

S4/5/6: He is famous/humorous/special in appearance.

T: Yes, Chaplin is humorous and special in appearance, and he is also a famous master around the world. Can you guess the meaning of "master"?

Ss: ...

T: "Master" means someone who is great in a special area, "大师" in Chinese. So here we can say, Chaplin is a master of nonverbal humor. Do you know the meaning of "nonverbal humor"? What is "nonverbal"?

Ss: ...

T: Nonverbal means without words. So nonverbal humor means acting a funny thing without words, just through body language.

【设计说明】 本环节要求学生利用视频以及文章的标题和图片展开头脑风暴,陈述关于 Chaplin 的已知信息,从而激活学生的已有图式。头脑风暴后,对标题关键字 master 和 nonverbal humor 的进一步理解能帮助学生更好地把握文章基调。

Step 2: While-reading (24 mins)

Activity 1. Skimming (3 mins)

Skim the passage and find out the information about Chaplin, and match the main idea of each paragraph.

Blank filling

Basic Information about Chaplin

Birth: _____
Death: _____
Type of acting: _____
Famous character: _____

Keys: 1889; 1977; mime; the tramp

Matching

Para. 1 → his popularity
Para. 2 → his achievements and people's love towards him
Para. 3 → his childhood
Para. 4 → his famous character
Para. 5 → an example of his work

T: Today, we are going to learn more about Chaplin and find out why he is called a master of nonverbal humor. Here is some basic information about Chaplin, such as his dates of birth and death, his type of acting and his famous character. Please skim the passage quickly and fill in the chart.

Ss：...

T： OK，let's check the answer. As we can see，there are five paragraphs in this passage，I've already showed the main idea of each paragraph，please match them together quickly.

Ss：...

【设计说明】 该活动旨在要求学生运用略读和找读找出文章信息，从而锻炼其阅读技能。找出 Chaplin 的基本信息能够让学生对他有进一步了解，而段落大意的连线能够让学生对文章的结构更加清晰，从而帮助学生进一步理解文章内容。

Activity 2. Careful reading (21 mins)

Para. 1 — Charlie Chaplin's popularity (3 mins)

Read Para. 1，and answer the questions：

Q1： What was the life background of people living at that time? How did they feel?

Q2： Why do you think Chaplin was popular at that time?

Q3： What is the element leading to Chaplin's mastery of acting?

T： After the reading，can you find the life background of people living at that time?

S7： At the time of two world wars.

T： How did they feel?

S8： Depressed. /Sad.

T： Yes，people were depressed，so in such situation，why do you think Chaplin was popular at that time?

S9/10/11： He made people laugh. /He brightened the lives of American and British people. /He made people feel more content with their lives.

T： Great. Chaplin made people laugh and feel more content with their lives，so people love him. From this paragraph，what is the element leading to Chaplin's mastery of acting?

S12/13： One need to be loved by people/need to do something for the society.

T： Yes，Chaplin brought laughter and hope for people at that time，so it means one should make contribution to others to make himself a master.

【设计说明】 在精读阶段，之所以对文章进行逐段阅读，除了可以降低学生的阅读难度之外，还便于学生更好地消化本堂课的教学重点，逐一概括每一段的段落大意，最终得出 Chaplin 成为大师的五要素。本环节的前两个展示性问题旨在让学生了解当时的历史背景和人们对 Chaplin 的态度，从而让学生理解 Chaplin 广受欢迎的原因。其次，通过第三个参考性问题，学生能够总结出 Chaplin 成为大师的要素之一是对社会有所贡献。

Para. 2 — Charlie Chaplin's childhood (4 mins)

Read Para. 2 and explain "astonishing" and "worse off", then answer the questions:

Q1: Is Charlie's own life easy? Can you find some supporting details?

Q2: Based on the details, what is the second element to make Chaplin a master?

Then Ss read the given sentence on the screen and find other similar sentences in the passage and later conclude the feature of these sentences and learn the figure of speech — litotes.

> **Explore Litotes (反叙)**
>
> **Nobody** has been able to do this better than Charlie Chaplin.
>
> =Everybody has been able to do this worse than Charlie Chaplin.
>
> Which one is better?
>
> Can you find more from Para. 1 & 2?

Keys: Not that Charlie's life was easy. No one was ever bored watching him.

T: Chaplin made people laugh at that time, but was his own life full of happiness since his childhood? Let's read Para. 2 and find out the answer.

Ss: ...

T: Was Chaplin's life easy?

S14: No, his life was not easy.

T: Why? Can you find some sentences to support your ideas?

S15: Because Charlie was taught to sing as soon as he could speak and dance as soon as he could walk.

S16: Charlie's father died when he was young, so he needed to take care of his family.

T: Nice answers. Since his life was difficult, did he give up?

Ss: No.

T: So we can see that Chaplin's life was not easy, but he overcame the difficulties and became a famous actor. According to his life experience, what made Charlie a master?

S17: One should be optimistic to be a master. Because even when Chaplin's family was poor, he didn't give up his life.

S18: One should have a determined mind. Because even during the hard times, Chaplin still didn't give up trying to be a good actor.

T: Yes. One step to be a master is to be optimistic, persistent and caring. Now let's look at this sentence: **Nobody** has been able to do this better than Charlie Chaplin. It means everybody has been able to do this worse than Charlie Chaplin. Can you find more similar sentences in Paragraph 1 - 2?

S19/20: Not that Charlie's life was easy. /No one was ever bored watching him.

T: What's the similarity among these sentences?

S21: They all begin with negative words such as "not", "nobody" and "no one".

T: Great. It is actually a kind of figure of speech called litotes, and it usually begins with a negative word to emphasize the mood of the sentence.

【设计说明】 根据句子"Not that Charlie's own life was easy",教师介绍了 Chaplin 童年的经历,让学生了解他所经历的困难。通过他青年时期的广受欢迎,学生能够总结出他的良好品质,同时也是他成为大师的要素之一,例如乐观坚强、照顾家人、坚忍不拔等。此外,本文修辞手法的运用是文章的亮点也是难点。在这一段中,教师让学生找出反叙的句子,通过举例对比和解释说明,让学生更好地体会其中的情感。

Para. 3 — Charlie Chaplin's famous character (3 mins)

Read Para. 3 and find out details about Chaplin's famous character, then answer the following questions:

Q1: What did he dress himself in? What was unusual about his outfit?

Q2: Why did he dress up like this?

Q3: Why did people like him?

Q4: What element can you infer to be a master from this paragraph?

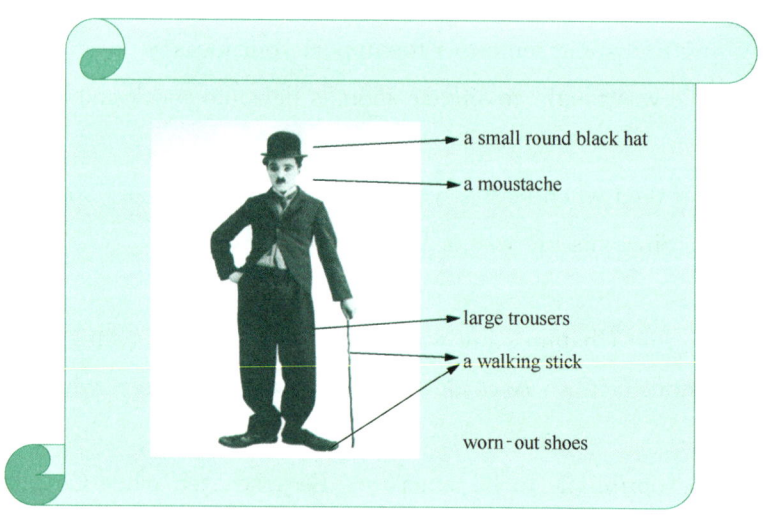

T: Read Para. 3, and find out what Chaplin's famous character is.

Ss: The little tramp.

T: The little tramp. It means "小流浪汉" in Chinese. What's the appearance of the little tramp?

S22: A small round black hat/a mustache/large trousers/a walking stick/worn-out shoes.

T: His outfit was quite special, right? Why do you think he dressed up like this?

Ss: ...

T: We can see that his clothes were tight, his trousers and shoes were not suitable for him, so it shows that he was poor. But he still wore a hat and carried a walking stick even if he was a social underdog, it shows his optimism towards life. From his dressing, can you tell the reason why people like him?

S23: People like him because of his determination and optimism.

T: From the little tramp's appearance and people's love towards him, can you conclude one element to become a master?

S24: One should create his own image to make himself special.

T: Yes, this means one should find a way that suits him best to be a master.

【设计说明】 与前两段的分析步骤相似,首先,依据小流浪汉的典型穿着,教师引导学生分析他如此穿着的原因,人们喜爱他的原因以及他的性格特征。该段的问题要求学生能够结合 Chaplin 的时代背景,分析推断原因,发展学生的评判性思维。同时,从 Chaplin 创造的经典形象得出 Chaplin 成功的要素之一是找到合适自身的发展之路。

Para. 4 — an example of Charlie Chaplin's work (8 mins)

Read Para. 4, and find out the basic information about the movie *The Gold Rush*, then understand the figure of speech — simile. Underline the verbs in this paragraph, and make a conversation with the verbs and act it out. After the acting, answer the questions:

Q1. How could Chaplin perform the little tramp so successfully?

Q2. Do you think the little tramp's childhood experience affected his acting?

Q3. Conclude one element to be a master from this paragraph.

The Gold Rush

Time: _____

Place: _____

Character: _____

Explore Simile（比喻）

He tries cutting and chewing the bottom of the shoe **as if** it were the finest steak.

He picks out the lace of the shoe and eats it **as if** it were spaghetti.

He is eating the noodles as if he _____.

She is crying as if she _____.

A Scene in *The Gold Rush*

Little Tramp: At last! Thank goodness! Somewhere to hide from the snow! We're lucky to find this hut before we disappeared under the snow.

Friend: Yes indeed. It's warm here but I'm hungry!

Little Tramp: Perhaps ...

T: No one can have an overnight success. Next, let's move on and enjoy one of his acting, find out the reason for his popularity. First, read Para. 4 and find the basic information about *The Gold Rush*, such as the time, the place and the character mentioned in the paragraph.

Ss: ...

T: An easy task, right? Now let's read more carefully. In this paragraph, there are many vivid verbs describing Chaplin's behavior, can you underline them?

Ss: pick out; eat; cut off; cut and chew.

T: Very good. Now please look at the three sentences describing his eating. The first two sentences both use "as if". They both used another figure of speech — simile. Could you guess the purpose of using simile?

S25: To make the article more vivid.

T: Yes, to make the passage more vivid and more attractive to readers. Now, can you use simile to make sentences of the pictures on the PPT?

Ss: ...

T: Good job. The writer used simile and many vivid verbs to describe the scene in the movie, but as we all know, *The Gold Rush* is a silent movie, so there were no dialogues. What dialogue do you think they might talk in this movie if it's not a silent one? Please work in groups and make your own dialogue with the verbs "pick out; eat; cut off; cut and chew". On the screen is the beginning of the dialogue. Have a discussion and act it out.

Ss: ...

T: Is it hard to act out how delicious the food is?

Ss: Yes.

T: So we can imagine that Chaplin must be a master to act without any words. Now, can you tell me why Chaplin could perform the little tramp so successfully?

S26: Because he is good at acting.

T: Do you think Charlies' childhood experience affected his acting?

Ss: ...

T: Because of his childhood, Chaplin understood life and people better than other performers, so he could act poor people really well. So from this paragraph, can you conclude one element to be a master?

Ss: ...

T: Yes, from this paragraph we can see that one's early experience and good skills contribute to his becoming a master.

【设计说明】 根据图式理论,读者和作者共享的图式越多,阅读理解就会越多。因此,阅读者只有在原有共享的图式基础上展开联想和猜测,不断激活相关的图式,并经过推理和判断,选择适合作者意图的图式,才能顺利完成阅读理解。教师要求学生依靠文本信息并发挥想象力,自己为电影设计对话脚本并进行表演,不仅能调动学生课堂积极性,还能引导学生学习人物动作描写的方法,更能让学生更好地理解 Chaplin 在表演这一幕时的精彩之处,从而自然而然地理解他为何被称为"大师",并得出成为大师所需的步骤之一是掌握良好的技能。与此同时,教师在本段介绍了另一种修辞手法——明喻,并指导学生看图造句,从而更好地掌握明喻,理解文章体现的情感色彩。

Para. 5 — Charlie Chaplin's achievement (3 mins)

Read Para. 5, and answer these questions:

Q1. What award did Chaplin win?

Q2. What was Chaplin except an actor? What else did he do?

Q3. What's the last step to be a master according to this paragraph?

T: According to the passage, what award did Chaplin win?

Ss: He won a special Oscar in 1972.

T: A special Oscar, very good. And here are some other awards he won. Except awards,

Chaplin had many different occupations other than acting. Can you find out what Chaplin did except acting?

Ss: He was also a writer/a director/a movie producer.

T: He wrote, directed, acted and produced the films, and he won a lot of awards. According to the information, can you find out the last step to be a master?

Ss: ...

T: It shows that one should have achievement in his career to be a master.

【设计说明】 本段中,教师先呈现了两个展示型问题来进一步分析卓别林,随后对他成功的最后一个要素进行总结,即在事业上有所成就,从而完成卓别林成为大师的五要素,完成文章框架搭建。

Step 3. Post-reading (10 mins)

Activity 1. Title understanding (2 mins)

Read the title again, and explain why Chaplin is called "the master of nonverbal humor".

T: After the reading, can you explain why Chaplin is a master of nonverbal humor?

S28: (He had good skills in performance, and he created his own character and it was famous all around the world.)

S29: (He had a lot of good qualities, such as being optimistic, persistent and caring.)

S30: (He had a lot of achievements in his own area, and won many awards.)

T: Chaplin's own life was not easy, but he still worked hard to deliver hope and laughter to people. That's why he is called a master of nonverbal humor.

【设计说明】 在阅读全文后,学生需要提取关键信息来理解文章标题,并回答相应的评价性问题。该评价性问题要求学生在分析和概括文章的基础上,结合文章信息和个人观点,从而给出答案,有利于发展学生的高层次思维能力。

Activity 2. Discussion (8 mins)

Conclude your own elements to be successful according to the enlightenment of five elements for Chaplin to become a master.

T: We call Chaplin a master because he is successful as an actor, and by reading the passage, we conclude five elements to be a master. Now, think about what elements do you think you should have if you want to be successful, and design your own 5 elements to be successful. Share your opinions with your classmates and explain your reasons.

Ss: ...

【设计说明】 依据Chaplin成为大师的五要素,学生需要通过小组讨论,写出自己成功的五要素。在布鲁姆的教育目标分类学中,这类活动属于评价层面,需要学生结合文章内容和自身特点,将Chaplin成为大师的五要素进行总结与转化,最终运用于自己的人生道路,旨在升华主题,发展学生的高阶思维能力。

Conclusion

T: Today we learned something about Charlie Chaplin, a master of nonverbal humor. He is charming, popular and attractive. He is also optimistic, persistent and caring. I hope all of you can learn something from him, and always remember to be optimistic and persistent no matter what difficulties you meet with. Because this is the only path to success, just as Charlie Chaplin was. You are an ordinary person, but you can do extraordinary work.

2. 板书设计

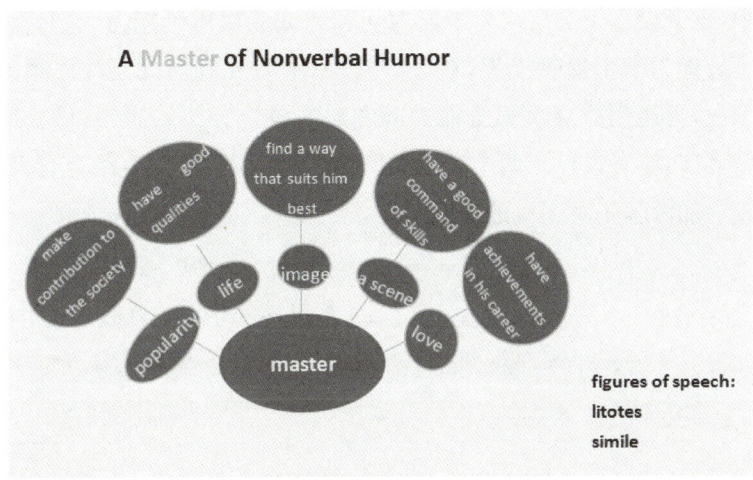

3. 作业布置(2分钟)

再次观看小面包舞,以文章第四段为例,对Chaplin的动作进行细节描述。在写作中,尽可能运用课堂中所学的修辞手法。文章长度为60字左右。

【设计说明】 作为《淘金记》中的著名片段,小面包舞展现了Chaplin的精湛演技。该作业旨在要求学生对课堂所学的修辞手法进行练习,并进一步感受小流浪汉的魅力之处。

(三) 教学反思

本节课旨在让学生充分利用阅读技巧分析解读文本,掌握反叙与比喻等修辞手法,理解Chaplin之所以被称为"幽默大师"的原因,并阐释自己对于成功的理解,发现自身的成功之路。为达到以上目的,笔者做了以下几点:

1. 明确主线,搭建文章框架,深化文章主题

以Chaplin成为大师的五要素为主线,整节课分为三个阶段(读前、读中和读后),每个阶段联系紧密,为分析文章搭建了清晰的框架。课堂以学生为中心,在结束每一段的阅读后,

教师均会要求学生自己总结 Chaplin 成为大师的要素。同时,读后讨论环节的设置进一步巩固了教学重点,并提供平台让学生能够进一步了解并设计自己成功的五要素,从而升华文章主旨,有助于学生高层次思维能力的发展。

2. 突破难点,通过多样化的方式学习修辞手法

修辞手法是增加文本表达效果的常用手段之一,教材中修辞的运用并不少见。但是,在课堂教学中,教师往往会轻视对修辞手法的讲解。作为本文的难点,笔者将修辞手法的学习融入文本分析中,通过举例对比、图片展示、造句等方法解释和练习修辞手法的使用,从而让学生在掌握修辞的基础上,更好地了解文章的情感色彩,感受 Chaplin 之所以受人敬仰,被称为"幽默大师"的原因。

3. 问题层次明确,为学生准确解读课文搭建支架

在本节课中,笔者设置了高层次思维能力问题和低层次思维能力问题,从而逐步推进文本解读。为了更好地为学生提供支架,在读中阶段,笔者先利用低层次思维能力问题,帮助学生寻找文本信息,再运用高层次思维能力问题对文章进行深入思考,做到基于文本,又高于文本。在读后环节,笔者设计了两个高层次思维能力问题,让学生结合自身来谈谈成功之路,突出教学重点,加深学生对主旨的理解。

(教学设计撰写:浙江大学附属中学 倪晗)

教材文本

A Master of Nonverbal Humor

As Victor Hugo once said, "Laughter is the sun that drives winter from the human face", and up to now nobody has been able to do this better than Charlie Chaplin. He brightened the lives of Americans and British through two world wars and the hard years in between. He made people laugh at a time when they felt depressed, so they could feel more content with their lives.

Not that Charlie's own life was easy! He was born in a poor family in 1889. His parents were both poor music hall performers. You may find it astonishing that Charlie was taught to sing as soon as he could speak and dance as soon as he could walk. Such training was common in acting families at this time, especially when the family income was often uncertain. Unfortunately, his father died, leaving the family even worse off, so Charlie spent his childhood looking after his sick mother and his brother. By his teens, Charlie had, through his humor, become one of the most popular child actors in England. He could mime and act the fool doing ordinary everyday tasks. No one was ever bored watching him — his subtle acting made everything entertaining.

As time went by, he began making films. He grew more and more popular as his charming character, the little tramp, became known throughout the world. The tramp, a poor, homeless man with a moustache, wore large trousers, worn-out shoes and a small round black hat. He walked around stilly carrying a walking stick. This character was a social failure but was loved for his optimism and determination to overcome all difficulties. He was the underdog who was kind even when others were unkind to him.

How did the little tramp make a sad situation entertaining? Here is an example from one of his most famous films, *The Gold Rush*. It is the mid-nineteenth century and gold has just been discovered in California. Like so many others, the little tramp and his friend have rushed there in search of gold, but without success. Instead they are hiding in a small hut on the edge of a mountain during a snowstorm with nothing to eat. They are so hungry that they try boiling a pair of leather shoes for their dinner. Charlie first picks out the laces and eats them as if they were spaghetti. Then he cuts off the leather top of the shoe as if it were the finest steak. Finally he tries cutting and chewing the bottom of the shoe. He eats each mouthful with great enjoyment. The acting is so convincing that it makes you believe that it is one of the best meals he has ever tasted!

Charlie Chaplin wrote, directed and produced the films he starred in. In 1972 he was given a special Oscar for his outstanding work in films. He lived in England and the USA but spent his last years in Switzerland, where he was buried in 1977. He is loved and remembered as a great actor who could inspire people with great confidence.

说课案例七（读写课）

PEP NSEFC M6 U3 Advice from Grandad (Reading and writing)

Good morning, everyone! I'm XX from XXXX. It's my great honor to be here to present my lesson plan. This is a reading and writing class. The material adopted here is from NSEFC Module 6 Unit 3 *A Healthy Life*, the reading part, with the title of *Advice from Grandad*, telling a Grandfather's

微课

great efforts to persuade his grandson to quit smoking.

Ⅰ. Analysis

The whole passage is made up of five paragraphs. The first paragraph tells the healthy life granddad led, whose intention is to be used as an example to persuade his grandson to quit smoking. It is easy to summarize the main idea, but it is not easy to infer the intention. In Paragraph Two, granddad gives his opinions on smoking, saying it is tough to quit. In Paragraph Three, granddad lists three aspects of how people get addicted to smoking. Since the students have already mastered some basic reading skills, such as skimming and scanning, it is easy for them to locate those three aspects as "physically", "through habit", and "mentally". And in Paragraph Four, granddad gives some harmful effects of smoking both on smokers and non-smokers. And in Paragraph Five, there is an attachment from the Internet as granddad's advice.

The whole passage is a good choice to train students' summarizing skills for the following reasons: for one thing, the whole passage is clearly structured and logically written; for another, the language is vivid and easy to understand.

Ⅱ. Statement

After analyzing the background of my lesson plan, the teaching objectives will be presented as follows. After this lesson, firstly, the students will be able to learn and use the important words and expressions, such as *tough* and *quit*, and later use these words to summarize the main idea of each paragraph, which is also the focus of this lesson. Secondly, students will be able to use the conjunctions, such as *firstly* and *secondly*, to integrate the main idea of each paragraph by themselves. Thirdly, students will be able to know the harmful effects of smoking on people's life as well as their health, and the importance of a healthy life. Meanwhile, they will be able to set up the framework and accomplish the writing by themselves.

In order to achieve the above objectives, the whole lesson will adopt the bottom-up teaching mode so that students can summarize the main idea of each paragraph first, and later integrate them in a whole.

Ⅲ. Description

With the analysis and the statement of my lesson plan mentioned above, here comes my teaching procedure. The whole lesson will be divided into four steps, as the first step to get the basic information of the whole passage, the second step to get the detailed information as well as the main idea of each paragraph, the third step to set up the framework and accomplish the first writing, and the last step to appreciate and evaluate the first writing. And then, I will describe my procedure in detail.

Step one: checking to find the basic information. The students are supposed to read the passage before the class. And in this part, several questions based on "who", "what" "why", and "how" are listed to help them get the basic information, such as the question "From whom to whom was the letter written?" With the previous reading skills, some questions are easy for them to answer while others are not that easy for them to express accurately, such as the question " How did Granddad persuade?" Students may give me the answer like "Grandad wrote this letter to persuade", which is not that accurate. So with this question, we will switch to step two.

Step two: careful reading. This step consists of two activities. Activity one: finding the topic sentences and key words. The students are supposed to read carefully and try to pick out the topic sentences and key words of each paragraph. Since the topic sentence of each paragraph is clear, it's easy to locate the key words, as we can see on the blackboard.

Activity two, summarizing the main idea of each paragraph. Here, I will lead the students to analyze paragraph by paragraph carefully, list some questions for their better understanding, and then summarize the main ideas one by one. In Paragraph one, I will ask them "Why did Granddad list his healthy life?". Students may give me the answer like "to persuade". In this way, the students get to know the writer's purpose of writing this letter. And later, they can summarize Paragraph One as "In order to persuade his grandson to quit smoking, granddad took his own healthy life as an example". For Paragraph 2, I will ask them the function of this paragraph. Most students can give me the answer like "It's a transitional paragraph". And for Paragraph 3, I will ask them "What are the ways in which people get addicted to smoking?". With their previous reading skills, it is easy for them to locate those three aspects. But those three aspects were not consistent in form, so I will guide them to turn "through habits" into "habitually". In this way, the students can get to know the main idea of Paragraph Three as "People can get addicted to smoking physically, habitually and mentally". And for Paragraph 4, I will ask them some questions based on "harmful effects", and I will ask them "Does smoking only affect the smokers?", of course students can get the answer like "Smoking affects people on both smokers and non-smokers" and then I will ask them "Does smoking affect people only in one aspect?", and they will give the answer like "Smoking affects both people's health and life". So in this way, the students can summarize the main idea of Paragraph Four as "Smoking can affect both smokers and non-smokers in every aspect of their health and their life". And for

Paragraph 5, some questions based on the advice are put forward, such as "Where is the advice?". Students can get the answer like "The advice is attached to the letter". So from the attached advice, students could get to know the great efforts Granddad tried to persuade his grandson. To sum up, locating each topic sentence is not hard, but summarizing the main idea in the students' own words is. In this way, students can get the main idea of each paragraph accurately and concisely, which lays a solid foundation for the writing part.

And now here comes my third step: accomplishing the first writing. In this part, I will provide them with a table as a basic framework with some conjunctions such as "firstly" and "secondly", and they ought to integrate the main ideas they have summarized before and accomplish the summary in a logical way by themselves. By doing so, they are able to express themselves logically and coherently.

All things getting ready, here comes my last step, appreciating the first writing. Here, I will present students an example of the summary for them to evaluate and I will ask them to judge from the following aspects: content, language and structure. Students should consider:

① Are all the elements mentioned?

② Is there any mistake in the language?

③ Are they logical?

Some students may not be likely to evaluate accurately and even don't dare to open their mouth to say something, so I will invite one of the top students to air his opinion first, setting an example for other students. With these criteria, the students will be able to reflect on their own writing and revise it later.

IV. Exposition

Now, here comes my homework. My homework today can be divided into two types: Must and Optional. For the former one, students are supposed to polish their summary writing and hand in the next day, which is a good way to examine their understanding of this class and also leaves them more time to reflect and think. For the latter one, the students are supposed to surf the Internet and try to find out more ways of quitting smoking, which is of great help to cultivate students' autonomous learning ability.

Here is my blackboard design, which could best show my lesson plan for this class. The basic structure of this passage is also shown on the blackboard.

V. Reflection

In conclusion, since reading serves as language input and writing functions as language output, a comprehensive input can guarantee an effective output. So the shining points of my lesson can be concluded as follows. On the one hand, all the reading activities are based on one topic, where language, structure and content are prepared, and the writing part is designed to examine students' understanding. On the other hand, the teaching objectives are clear, with questions driven to deal with the focus and difficulties.

That's all for my lesson plan presentation. Thanks for your attention.

（说课稿撰写：温州第二高级中学　王旭碧）

附：教学设计及教材文本

M6 U3 Advice from Grandad

（一）教学分析

1. 教材分析

本节课的教材选自人教版《普通高中课程标准实验教科书英语选修 6》第三单元 *A Healthy Life* 的阅读部分，阅读语篇名为 *Advice from Granddad*。该语篇以书信形式为主，讲述了一位爷爷苦口婆心、以身为戒，劝导其孙子戒掉烟瘾。书信中讲述了吸烟的危害，故本文的主要脉络为爷爷如何劝说孙子戒掉烟瘾。文本主要以书信的形式呈现，段落写作结构和逻辑清晰，后三段关键词明显，故学生可以通过关键词及相应的细节信息概括段落大意。信的内容共分为五个段落，分别从爷爷自身的健康生活、戒烟的难度、烟瘾的三种表现、烟瘾带来的危害及如何戒烟的建议来劝说其孙子戒烟。结构虽然清晰容易理解，但文章第一段的写作意图难以推测，第二段的作用难以分析，第三段 physically、through habit 和 mentally 三个词的词性不一致，学生难以归纳概括，这就需要教师进一步的引导。根据词性一致原则，教师可通过把"through habit"转换成"habitually"，来培养学生语言转述能力，发展学生思维，扫除学生的语言障碍，帮助学生近一步了解文本。戒烟这一话题对于大部分学生来说可能比较乏味，但这封信的语言生动、难度适中，能够吸引学生的注意力，激起学生的学习兴趣。因此，在教学过程中，教师可以针对主要信息提出问题，便于学生分辨主、次要信息，快速找到关键词、概括段落大意，然后根据自己的理解用简洁明了的话语整合整个段落。

2. 学情分析

本课学生为浙江省某重点高中高二学生，男生 18 人，女生 32 人。他们所使用的教材为人教版高中英语必修和选修部分，他们已有较好的英语学习方法及良好的英语学习基础，平时学生的课堂多为中英文双语教学。学生的具体学习情况如下：

阅写技能方面：学生早已掌握一些阅读的技巧，如 skimming 和 scanning、根据上下文猜测文本中新词的意思，并且能根据信中出现的细节信息简单地概括每一段的段落大意。但是学生仍然无法全面且精确地找出每一段的关键信息，故难以准确地进行概括。在信息整合和框架搭建方面，学生仍缺乏一定的语篇逻辑性和连贯性，难以顺利梳理信息、自主地搭建概要写作框架。通过本节课的学习，学生能够学会批判性地阅读寻找主、次要信息，并通过表格形式搭建框架。

思维能力方面：日常写作中，学生偏向于拿到题目便开始书写，缺乏写作前谋篇布局的习惯，这种边写边思考的习惯容易导致写作结果过于碎片化。通过本节课的学习，学生能够学会批判性地阅读和逻辑性地书写，通过分析、推断、综合、归纳、概括等能力的培养，促进其思维能力的发展。

学习习惯方面：本班大部分学生比较内向，他们不喜欢小组讨论或者协作学习，故本节课主要以学生单独回答和书面表达为主，以此来满足学生的学习和认知方面的需求。

3. 教学目标

（1）语言能力：基于文本，寻找关键词，用自己的话语概括段落大意；掌握以下词汇的运用，如 quit，be addicted to，tough，physically 和 mentally 等等。

（2）思维品质：通过连接词的使用，达到概要写作语篇衔接的逻辑性要求。

（3）文化意识：了解人们染上烟瘾的原因以及吸烟对人类生活的影响；知道戒烟与保持健康生活的重要性，对生活持有积极的态度。

（4）学习能力：学会自主的进行阅读、通过关键词和主题句搭建写作框架。

4. 教学重难点

基于问题驱动，学生能够准确找出每一段的关键词，概括每一段的段落大意，搭建概要写作的框架。（重点）

文章第一段的写作意图难以推测，第二段文本的作用难以分析，第三段 physically、through habit 和 mentally 三个词的词性不一致，学生难以归纳。（难点）

5. 教学思路

本堂课教学内容主要围绕爷爷劝导孙子戒烟的线索，爷爷以自身的健康生活为案例，分别从戒烟难、烟瘾的三种表现、烟瘾的危害及戒烟的建议这几个角度进行劝说。本堂课共设四个步骤（见图1）：一读检查，提取表层信息；细节研读，深入挖掘文本；框架搭建，撰写概要初稿；范文评鉴，修改润色定稿。本文主要采取问题驱动模式教学对本文内容进行深入的分析，预设问题，以此来帮助学生快速获取关键信息，搭建概要写作框架。在热身部分，教师通过设置四个问题核查学生的预习情况，帮助学生梳理文本的基本信息；在阅读部分，教师首先引导学生寻找每段的关键词，然后分五部分阅读寻找具体的细节信息，引导学生用自己的话语概括段落大意；在书写部分，学生在理顺文本思路之后，独立完成概要写作初稿；写后进行鉴赏，核查内容覆盖是否全面，语篇是否具有逻辑性和语言是否连贯。

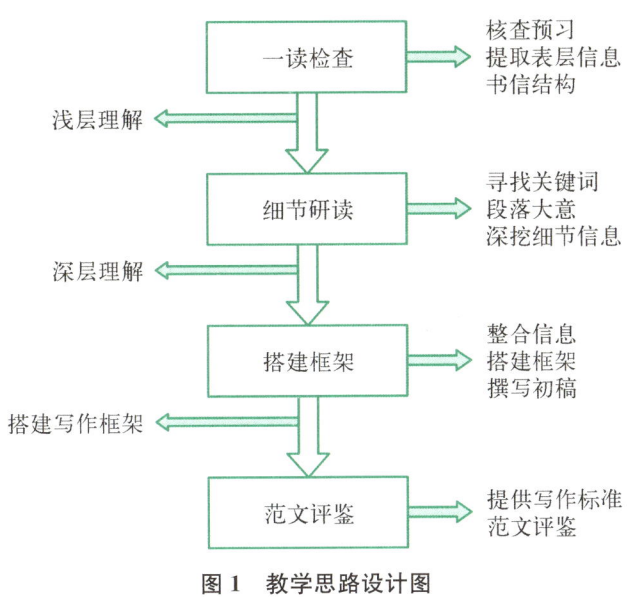

图 1 教学思路设计图

(二) 教学过程

1. 教学活动

步骤一. 一读检查,提取表层信息(4 mins)

Students are supposed to read the material before the class and then during the checking part, they are supposed to answer several questions to check whether they have got to know the basic information of this passage.

Q1: From whom to whom was the letter written?

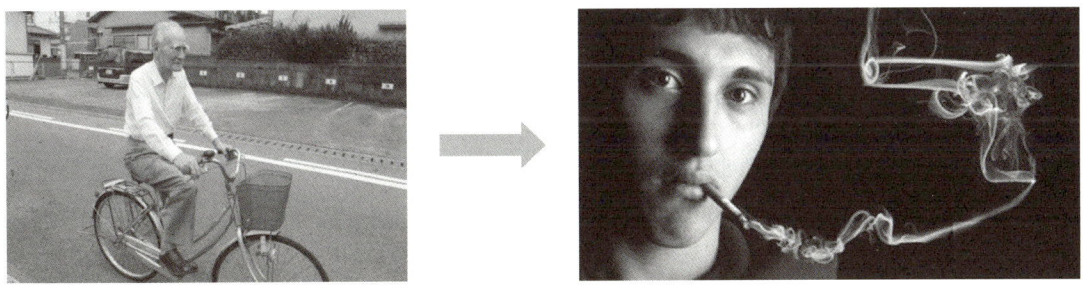

Q2: What is written in this letter?

Q3: What's the purpose of writing this letter?

A. To inform. B. To persuade.

C. To argue. D. To explain.

Q4: How did the granddad persuade his grandson?

T: Good morning, everyone. Have you read the passage on your textbook?

97

Ss: Yes.

T: Very good. Now let's check whether you have got the basic information of this passage after your first reading. First, who wrote this letter and who was this letter written to?

S1: This letter was written by James's grandfather to James.

T: That's right. From James' granddad to James. And what's written in the letter?

S2: The ways people become accustomed to smoking and the harm of smoking.

T: Cool, you have almost mentioned all. Next, why did the author write this letter? Or we can say the purpose of this letter? You can choose one.

S3: B. To persuade.

T: Yes, to persuade. So how did granddad persuade his grandson not to smoke?

S4: He wrote this letter to persuade.

T: That's it. What else?

S5: He told James the reasons why it was tough to quit and why it was harmful to smoke and then gave him some advice.

T: Wow, it seems that you have a basic information of this passage. And now let's read for the second time. And see exactly how he tried to persuade James.

【设计意图】 提问是核查学生是否获得书信基本信息的最佳方式之一。通过这些问题,学生能够大致梳理这封信的结构,为第二次阅读做铺垫。题1的答案从标题即可猜测得出;题2是对全文的主旨的概括,因为课前已布置学生进行阅读,故即使没有选项,学生也能进行描述;题3是对这篇书信目的的阐释;题4是对表层信息的搜索。通过梯度不一的问题设置,促进学生不同层次的思考,有利于发展学生的思维品质。

步骤二. 细节研读,深入挖掘文本(20 mins)

活动一. 快速阅读,寻找关键词

After the checking part, students are supposed to read carefully and try to pick out the key words of each paragraph.

- Para. 1: (a healthy life)
- Para. 2: (tough to quit)
- Para. 3: (addicted)
- Para. 4: (harmful effects)
- Para. 5: (advice)

T: Have you finished your reading?

Ss: Yes.

T: Now please pick out the key words of each paragraph and try to circle the words that represent the main idea of each paragraph. So for the first paragraph?

S6: A healthy life.

T: That's right. And for Paragraph 2?

S7: It's tough to quit smoking.

T: Yes. And Paragraph 3?

S8: Addicted.

T: Yes, four?

S9: Harmful effect of smoking.

T: Great. So it talks about the harmful effect, right? And the last paragraph?

S10: Advice from granddad.

T: Excellent. Now you have got the key words of each paragraph. Very good. Those key words will help us to get the main idea of each paragraph and help us get a better understanding of the structure of this letter.

【设计意图】 在第一次阅读的基础上,教师引导学生进一步阅读,寻找每一段的关键词,如第一段的关键词就是爷爷的 a healthy life,第二段为 tough to quit,第三段为 addicted 等,这些关键词都是文本中直接可以找到的,降低了学生的学习难度。实际上,学生找到的关键词会比较多,教师需要引导其分辨主、次要信息。通过寻找关键词,学生能更好地理清文本结构,为后续搭建概要写作框架打下基础。

活动二. 段落研读,寻找细节信息,概括段落大意(20 mins)

In this part, the material is divided into five parts and students are supposed to read one paragraph by one paragraph, trying to answer the questions listed forward, and summarize the main idea of each paragraph according to the key information found in that paragraph.

Para. 1: A healthy life

Q1: Why did granddad list his healthy life?

Q2: What's the main idea?

T: Well, we know Paragraph 1 is about "a healthy life". So what is talked about in the first paragraph? Can you give me some key words?

S11: Fit enough, long and active life.

T: Yes, that's what you found. Great. So what does Paragraph 1 mainly talk about?

S11: It mainly talks about that granddad is healthy enough to do lots of things and live a long and active life.

T: That is to say, the importance of a healthy life, right?

S11: Yes.

T: So do you know the purpose of presenting his own healthy life?

S12: To ask his grandson to learn from him.

T: Yes, maybe.

S13: Persuade his grandson to quit smoking and form a good habit of a healthy life.

T: Wow, that's it. So that's the purpose of writing this letter, right? After knowing the writer's purpose, can you tell me the main idea of this paragraph?

S14: In order to persuade his grandson to quit smoking, the granddad used his own healthy life as an example.

Para. 2: Tough to quit smoking

Q1: What's the function of the second paragraph?

Q2: What's the main idea?

T: So after reading Paragraph 2, have you got the problem of James?

Ss: He started smoking and found it difficult to quit.

T: Good, so how to quit smoking is the problem that troubles James. So what's the function of the second paragraph?

S15: It's a transitional paragraph. And it also presents the purpose of this letter.

T: So the main idea of this paragraph is?

S15: It is tough to quit smoking.

Para. 3: Addicted

Q1: What are the ways in which people can become addicted to cigarettes? And how?

Degree	Things
physically	withdrawal symptoms, bad-tempered and sometimes even in pain
through habit (habitually)	do it automatically
mentally	happier and more relaxed, could only feel good when I smoked

Q2: What's the main idea of Paragraph 3?

T: Now, can you find the words that represent the time sequence?

Ss: Firstly, secondly and lastly.

T: Great. So we know there are three different ways in which people become addicted to cigarettes, right? So what are they? Please fill in the blanks on the screen.

S16: Physically addicted, through habit and mentally addicted.

T: That's right. And here we can see that through habit is quite different from the other two in form, can you change it into another word that is consistent with physically and mentally?

S16: Habitually.

T: Wonderful. And now please summarize the main idea of Paragraph 3.

S17: People can become addicted to smoking physically, mentally and habitually.

Para. 4: Harmful effects

Q1: Does smoking only affect the smokers?

Q2: Does smoking affect people only in one aspect?

Q3: What effects does smoking bring to people? Please list in details and then try to divide them into several aspects.

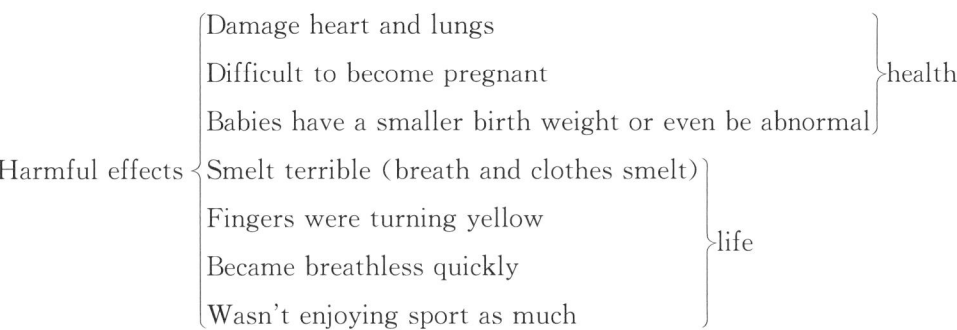

Q4: What's the main idea?

T: Now, read Paragraph 4 very quickly and try to answer these questions: Does smoking only affect the smokers? Does smoking affect people only in one aspect? And try to list some detailed information of how people are affected. OK, for the first one. Yes or no?

S18: No, it also affects the non-smokers.

T: Exactly. Smoking affects not only the smoker himself, but also the non-smokers. And what about the second one? Yes or no?

S19: No.

T: The answer is "no", right? How many kinds of effect have you found?

S20: The first thing is that it damages our heart and lungs, and it's difficult to get pregnant, and babies have a smaller birth weight or even be abnormal. Besides, smoking makes one smell terrible with fingers turning yellow, and become breathless quickly and can't enjoy sport much.

T: Great. So can you classify these effects?

S21: I think, the first three belongs to the effects on health, and the rest belongs to the effects on life.

T: That's right. So now can you summarize the main idea of this paragraph?

S22: Smoking affects both smokers and non-smokers on their health as well as life.

Para. 5: Advice

Teacher asks students to read Paragraph 5 carefully and answer the following questions:

Q1: Where does the advice come from?

Q2: Is the advice listed in the letter?

Q3: What does "so" mean in this paragraph?

Q4: What is the main idea of Paragraph 5?

T: For the last paragraph, the granddad sent his grandson some advice, so where did the advice come from?

S23: The advice was found on the internet.

T: Yes, and is the advice listed in the letter? Yes or no?

S24: No, it isn't. Maybe granddad sent it together with the letter.

T: Cool. Maybe the advice was listed in another document, right?

S24: Yes.

T: So it is attached. And do you know what the word "so" refer to? And what is the meaning?

S25: "So" means granddad wanted James to stop smoking and strengthen his resolve of quitting smoking.

T: Excellent, that's it.

S25: It expresses granddad's worry towards James' smoking.

T: Yes, maybe granddad is worried about James' health, right? So now can you summarize the main idea of this paragraph?

S26: Granddad attached some advice on quitting smoking.

【设计意图】 该环节中,教师将阅读文本分为五个部分进行分析,分别介绍爷爷如何劝说孙子James戒烟的经过。第一段中通过Why did granddad list his healthy life? 引导学生思考作者写第一段的真正意图;第二段中通过What's the function of the second paragraph? 引导学生探索第二段的作用,承上启下,衔接第一段和第三段;第三段通过What are the ways in which people can become addicted to cigarettes? 引导学生梳理该段的关键信息;第四段通过Does smoking only affect the smokers? Does smoking affect people only in one aspect? What effects does smoking bring to people? 这三个递进的问题链整合文本关键信息,学生能找到smokers和non-smokers,health和life这两个方面,以及具体影响人身体健康的例子;第五段通过Where does the advice come from? Is the advice listed in the letter? 引导学生对爷爷的建议是否在信中提及进行区分,为学生概括段落大意提供支撑。学生根据教师设置的围绕主题的问题链能够更全面理解文本,在每一个段落里教师都设置了对段落大意的归纳,引导学生一步步地进行文本内容概括。通过一段一段分析,学生的注意力会更集中在课堂任务上,能更准确地回答问题。此外,学生不仅能概括每一段的段落大意,为后面的概括做铺垫,还能搭建概要写作的框架,为后面的"写"做好准备。

步骤三. 框架搭建,撰写概要初稿(10 mins)

After analyzing each paragraph, students need to organize the structure of this letter and try to put them in a logical way. And they are supposed to integrate the main ideas they have summarized before and write the summary individually.

Purpose	To persuade his grandson to quit smoking.
How	**First,** his own experience **Second,** why it is tough to quit **Third,** people get addicted to smoking physically, mentally and habitually **Fourth,** why it is harmful to smoke **Lastly,** some advice

T: Well, before writing, let's make it much clearer. So we have known that the purpose of this letter is ...

Ss: To persuade his grandson to quit smoking.

T: Good. And how does grandpa persuade his grandson to stop smoking?

S27: He told his own healthy life. He explained why it is tough to quit smoking. He described how people get addicted to smoking physically, mentally and habitually.

T: Good, now since you have got the main idea of each paragraph, please try to integrate those main ideas into one summary with the help of the linking words.

Ss: ...

【设计意图】 通过表格的形式重新回顾文本信息有利于学生理清思路,在脑海中形成更直观的支架,构建概要框架。学生原本认为概要写作难度较大,这一环节降低了概要写作的难度。学生能自主地根据先前得到的信息进行整合,通过连接词 first、second、third、fourth 和 lastly 的呈现,使学生对这些信息的结构更清晰,更富有逻辑性,有利于学生的口头阐述和书面表达。在此基础上,学生能够更快更好地完成概要写作初稿。

步骤四. 范文评鉴,修改润色定稿(6 mins)

After writing, the teacher presents an example for students to evaluate and some criteria are also listed for students to judge whether it is good or not.

① Are all the elements mentioned?

② Are they logical?

③ Is there any mistake in the language?

T: What do you think of his writing? Try to appreciate it in the following dimensions: first, are all the elements mentioned? Second, are they logical? Third, is there any mistake in the language?

S28: I think it includes all the key information, so it's good.

S29: I think the structure is clear and the information is listed in a logical way.

S30: ...

Example:
> To persuade his grandson to quit smoking, a grandpa first described his own healthy life as an example and then explained why it is tough to quit and why it is harmful. He said one can be addicted to smoking physically, mentally and habitually. He also stated that smoking can harmfully affect both smokers and non-smokers in every aspect of their health and life. Lastly, he attached some advice on quit smoking. (72 words)

【设计意图】 在完成概要写作之后,教师先给出写作评价标准,即写作内容的全面性、准确性和逻辑性,随后呈现范文,并邀请部分学生对范文内容和结构进行评价,分别从内容覆盖的全面性、语言的准确性和语篇衔接的逻辑性几个落脚点出发进行评价。通过从各个方面进行评价鉴赏,有利于学生培养自身的评鉴能力。在此基础上,学生能够参照评价范文时提及的问题反思自己的写作是否存在问题,从而进行修改润色。

2. 板书设计

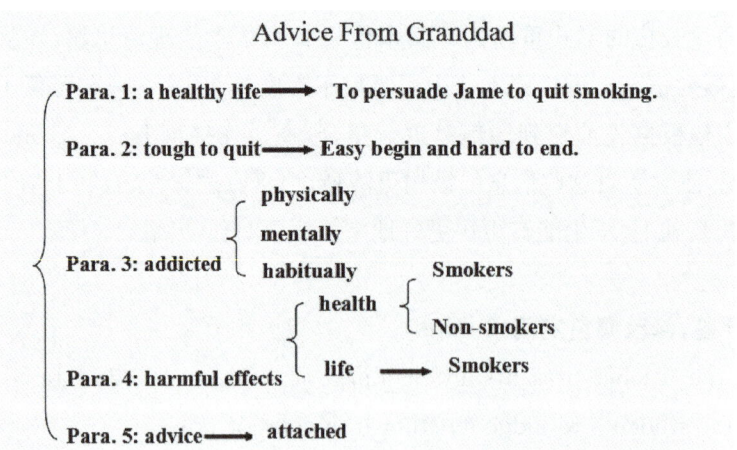

3. 作业布置(2 mins)

Must: Polish your summary writing and hand in tomorrow.

Optional: Surf the net and try to find some useful ways of quit smoking.

(三) 教学反思

概要写作是浙江省英语学科高考改革的重要题型。如何教会学生写好概要写作是高中英语教学中的一大难题。本节课主要包括读和写两部分,读为语言输入,而写则是语言产出。高效的输入有助于学生高质量的产出,高质量的产出又能促进学生更好地理解阅读材料,即以读促写,以写促读。本文旨在促进学生理解性地"读",逻辑性地"写",其教学亮点可分为以下两点。

1. 阅读服务于写作,写作检测阅读

本节课的所有阅读活动都是为了写作做准备。在阅读的过程中,学生通过对每一段段落大意的概括,获得了写作所需的内容、结构和语言。在此基础上,寻找各段落的关键信息,理清文章脉络和逻辑顺序,对概括的句子进行加工,分清主次关系,搭建概要写作的框架。所有的写作活动设计都是为了检测学生的阅读情况,如段落大意的整合等。

2. 目标明确,问题驱动,思维发展

本节课以核心素养的发展为主要教学目标,旨在培养学生的语言能力、思维品质、文化意识和学习能力,以"说"带"写",目标明确。以问题为驱动,教师在解读文本和设计问题的过程中旨在培养学生的读者意识,引导学生忠于原文的意识。在每一个段落分析中都设置了对段落大意的归纳,引导学生一步步地进行文本内容概括,增强阅读意识。此外,这些围绕主线"quit smoking"的问题链有助于学生思维的发展,尤其是逻辑思维的发展。

(教学设计撰写:温州第二高级中学　王旭碧)

教材文本

ADVICE FROM GRANDAD

Dear James,

  It's a beautiful day here and I am sitting under the big tree at the end of the garden. I have just returned from a long bike ride to an old castle. It seems amazing that at my age I am still fit enough to cycle 20 kilometres in an afternoon. It's my birthday in two weeks time and I'll be 82 years old! I think my long and active life must be due to the healthy life I live.

  This brings me to the real reason for my letter, my dear grandson. Your mother tells me that you started smoking some time ago and now you are finding it difficult to give up. Believe me, I know how easy it is to begin smoking and how tough it is to stop. You see, during adolescence I also smoked and became addicted to cigarettes.

By the way, did you know that this is because you become addicted in three different ways? First, you can become physically addicted to nicotine, which is one of the hundreds of chemicals in cigarettes. This means that after a while your body becomes accustomed to having nicotine in it. So when the drug leaves your body, you get withdrawal symptoms. I remember feeling bad-tempered and sometimes even in pain. Secondly, you become addicted through habit. As you know, if you do the same thing over and over again, you begin to do it automatically. Lastly, you can become mentally addicted. I believe I was happier and more relaxed after having a cigarette, so I began to think that I could only feel good when I smoked. I was addicted in all three ways, so it was very difficult to quit. But I did finally manage.

When I was young, I didn't know much about the harmful effects of smoking. I didn't know, for example, that it could do terrible damage to your heart and lungs or that it was more difficult for smoking couples to become pregnant. I certainly didn't know their babies may have a smaller birth weight or even be abnormal in some way. Neither did I know that my cigarette smoke could affect the health of non-smokers. However, what I did know was that my girlfriend thought I smelt terrible. She said my breath and clothes smelt, and that the ends of my fingers were turning yellow. She told me that she wouldn't go out with me again unless I stopped! I also noticed that I became breathless quickly, and that I wasn't enjoying sport as much. When I was taken off the school football team because I was unfit, I knew it was time to quit smoking.

I am sending you some advice I found on the Internet. It might help you to stop and strengthen your resolve. I do hope so because I want you to live as long and healthy a life as I have.

Love from
Grandad

第三部分 高中英语教研型说课案例

说课案例八（阅读课）

PEP NSEFC M4 U1 Women of Achievement

一、教学目标定位

各位老师，大家好！刚刚给大家呈现的阅读课选自人教版高中英语教材必修四第一单元 Women of Achievement。本课的阅读文本记叙了一位研究非洲猩猩的卓越女性 Jane Goodall 的人生经历。通过对 Jane 的介绍，本文表达了女性通过努力也可以取得甚至连男性都难以企及的成就，她们同样可以克服重重困难，为人类作出杰出的贡献。

本文标题是 A Student of African Wildlife，涵盖了故事中关于 who 和 what 的信息，用作读前预测文本内容，也用来读后分析 Jane 被称为 student 的原因。文本共分四段，分别介绍了 Jane 研究猩猩的方法、研究成果、研究目的以及 Jane 的成就。文中语言十分丰富，黑体词如 nest、outspoken 和 inspire 等词描述了猩猩的行为、Jane 的研究目的、研究方法和 Jane 的成就等。

基于上述分析，本堂课共提出 3 点语言技能和语言知识目标。首先，要求学生通过扫读、跳读等方式，快速获取文本相关信息，归纳整理 Jane 的研究方法、研究成果和研究目的。其次，在解读文本信息的过程中理解黑体词等词在上下文中的含义，理解 it all comes crowding in 中 it 的指代关系，以及 once you have seen that 中 that 的指代关系，并补全文中句子 You can never forget... 后面缺少的信息。最后，要求学生通过做笔记等方式，评价 Jane 的工作，思考 Jane 的为人，呈现自己对文本潜在意义的理解。

本课目标聚焦主要有三点，信息整理、语言处理和人物评价。虽然部分语言有一定难度，比如对于代词指代、有关省略的理解以及对人物的评价，但由于教学方法选择得当，教学活动设计合理，因此难点得到一一突破，教学目标得以顺利达成。

二、教学目标达成

具体教学环节不再赘述，这里我将重点说明本节课教学目标是如何达成的。首先，在一读中，教师引导学生从标题和图片出发，回答以下问题：1. What do you know about the animals in the pictures? 2. Who is the student? 3. What does the animal in the title refer to? 4. What else do you want to get from the passage?"一读"有助于理解文章大意,获取文本表层信息。通过标题和图片,引导学生预测文本内容;通过预测,提出阅读问题;通过阅读,学生获取 who、what 等相关信息。正如大家所见,该环节问题简单,答案易找,目标达成度高,耗时少,成效好。

在完成"一读"任务后,结合标题,提出问题,进行"二读"。二读聚焦的问题有 4 个: 1. How does she study the chimps? 2. Why does she study the chimps? 3. Why does the writer call Jane a student? 4. What is the writing purpose? 本课中,语言教学目标的达成贯穿始终,"一读"和"二读"侧重理解黑体词在文中的含义。"二读"还引导学生分析 Jane 被称为 student(学生)的原因,放手学生推测作者的写作意图,语言知识目标和阅读技能目标同时达成。

在完成文本内容和语言处理后,教师引导学生思考如下问题,进行"三读",评价人物: 1. What do you think of Jane? 2. What do you think of her work? 3. What does "it" refer to? 4. What does "that" refer to? 5. What can be possibly continued after "you can never forget…"? 基于对先前的文本解读,学生在评价 Jane 的工作和她的为人时有话可讲,有情可抒,评判性思维能力得到发展,教学目标的达成也落到了实处。"三读"还着重理清了文本中的指代关系,突破了省略造成的阅读障碍。当然,在语言课堂上,运用所学语言表达自己的观点应成为课堂教学的重要环节。因此,在本节课的最后阶段,教师带领学生对文本进行更为深入的解读,运用从文本获取的信息,使用课堂中所学的语言,发表自己的观点,分享各自的解读。此时的文本阅读,基于文本而又超越文本,作者的原意与学生的思想发生互动。正如大家所见,学生的评价是精彩的、独到的,学生对文本解读是有条理的、有层次的。

三、教学效果反思

本节研讨课旨在探讨如何将文本解读权放手交给学生,培养学生独立解读文本的能力。从教学效果看,本堂课基本达到了预期目标。反思本节课的教学设计与实施,有三点可取之处值得进一步探讨:1. 调控任务难度,给学生留出充分解读文本的时间;2. 巧妙设计问题,给学生搭建逐步解读文本的阶梯;3. 关注互动模式,给学生留下独立解读文本的机会。

(一)调控任务难度,给学生留出充分解读文本的时间,这是文本解读权利下放的前提。本节课采用互动教学模式,教师提出引导性问题,与学生互动,明确文本解读方向,然后放手学生自主解读文本。本堂课三个阅读环节的任务难度不同。"一读"任务比较简单,学生只需要根据教师要求,在文中找到相应的信息即可。这样的设计,在很大程度上保护了学生阅读的积极性,也为后续阅读奠定了基础。"二读"任务稍难,要求学生分析作者将 Jane 称为"student"的原因,并对文本的写作意图进行推测。本环节中,学生在文本中搜寻证据,对文本信息进行提炼与加工,难度较大。因此,教师给予学生足够的时间,适当降低对学生语言表达准确度的要求,适当提供帮助,以保证学生顺利完成任务。"三读"任务难度最大,要求学生基于全文理解,回答几个评估型问题,并且理解文中 it 和 that 的指代关系。学生在理解

it 和 that 指的是 chimps 在实验室和笼子里的情境后,学生才能根据对文本的理解,补全 You can never forget... 中的句子信息。虽然回答评估性问题不需要回读文本,但学生需要独立思考并组织语言表达自己的观点。因此,也要给予学生较多的思考时间,才能保证学生有较高质量的产出。

从本课的教学效果看,"三读"教学环节的设计安排,使学生拥有了充足的时间阅读全文,完成自己的文本解读。"三读"阅读问题的难度也是由小到大递增的,并且每个环节的教学目标不同,上一个环节教学目标的达成为下一次的阅读奠定了基础,这是一个循序渐进的过程。学生得以有时间深入思考、透彻研读,他们的解读才能更加从容、自信,效果才能更好。

(二)巧妙设计问题,给学生搭建逐步解读文本的支架,这是文本解读权利下放的关键。本堂课三个阅读环节的问题类型不同。"一读"重在教师引导,阅读问题属于封闭式的展示型问题,学生只要找到答案即可;"二读"重在学生归纳和推断,阅读问题属于半开放式的参考型问题,学生不仅要能找到信息,还要对信息进行提炼加工;"三读"重在提升,阅读问题主要属于开放式的评估型问题,另外"三读"还涉及了对文中重难点的突破和理解。

三个阅读环节不同类型的问题培养学生不同层次的思辨能力。在"一读"中,学生要做的是搜索信息和预测,属于较低层次思维的训练;"二读"中,学生要分析和推断,属于较高层次的思维训练;"三读"中学生要评价创造,属于高层次的思维训练。

在三个阅读环节中,问题的思维层次逐渐从低层次过渡到高层次,学生的思维能力也逐渐从低层次向高层次发展。这样的设计避免了学生直接面临高级思维问题的困难,让学生的思维有一个缓冲、适应、提升的过程,逐步提高学生思维的参与程度,为学生搭建了一个解读文本的支架。

(三)关注互动模式,给学生留下独立解读文本的机会,这是文本解读权利下放的保障。一般情况下,高中英语阅读课上学生的文本解读权十分有限,许多教师事必躬亲,精心设计阅读问题,还精心预设学生的答案。在这样的阅读课堂上,学生是被动的接受者,教师几乎剥夺了学生独立解读文本的机会。对于学生而言,要么完成任务无需思考,只需沿着教师的思路说出"教师"设定的答案即可,要么跟不上教师的解读思路和解读深度,只是简单理解或被动接受教师的解读。而本课中,正如大家所见,学生的参与是积极的,学生的产出是高效的,而这些效果得益于师生之间的有效互动,得益于给学生留出了自主解读文本的机会。

本节课中,在不同的阅读阶段,教师与学生互动的模式因不同类型、不同难度的文本解读问题而有所不同。"一读"过程中,教师的角色比较重要,把握文本的解读方向,布置阅读任务,提出阅读问题,学生的学习是在教师的指导下完成的;"二读"时,学生已经能够自主整理信息,对文本内容适当推断;"三读"时,学生已有个人观点的表达、有创造性的思维成果。后两遍阅读中,学生的解读越来越多,教师在教学过程中只是监听者和评价者。整个阅读课堂教师慢慢放手,学生逐渐独立、顺利地完成了文本解读任务。

当然,本课教学仍有一些改进的空间,阅读节奏把控仍有些不足,给学生的思考时间还可以更长,在评价 Jane 的为人时可以考虑给学生更多的机会。但这堂课也引发了我们更多的思考,高中英语阅读课可以通过分层阅读,逐渐放手由学生解读文本,培养学生独立解读文本的习惯和能力,促进学生评判性思维能力的提高。以上是我对这堂课的反思,不足之处还请各位老师批评、指正。

(说课稿撰写:浙江师范大学　杨聪聪　温州第二中学　项纸陆)

附:教学课例及教材文本

M4U1 Women of Achievement

一、课例背景

近年来,深入解读阅读文本成为趋势。备课要深入解读文本,课堂要落实解读要点,课后要反思解读有效性。解读深入人心,教师们研究文本解读理论,探讨文本解读的视角,反思文本解读的教学案例。我们欣然地发现,教师的课堂因文本解读而改变:文本解读更加多元,教学设计更有层次,阅读问题更加针对,学生活动更加丰富。但是,在取得可观的教学成果后,我们也发现了不少问题。首先,教师的解读是基于教师良好的语言能力、分析能力、组织能力,但是学生受其语言能力、思维能力的限制,无法完成教师布置的解读任务。另外,教师的解读往往是基于多次反复的文本解读,他们的解读往往是深入的、细致的,而学生受课堂时间的限制、教学任务的限制,没有那么多的机会完成解读。当然,教师的解读往往也会因为其个人的教学经验、人生阅历、阅读习惯等限制,提出纯粹基于个人理解的解读,因此导致学生无法根据文本完成同样的解读。

所以,我们往往看到这样的现象:教师为了完成教学预设,不得不"赶着"学生阅读文本、完成解读、回答问题。在此过程中,学生根本没有时间阅读,没有时间思考,更谈不上深入理解,课堂因此常常出现问题无人回答,师生长时间沉默的现象。而教师只能呈现自己的解读结果,或是告之阅读问题答案。一言蔽之,阅读文本解读似乎走了另一个极端,教师解读深入,学生解读仓促,学生的阅读课堂成为教师个人的"解读秀"。缺少时间的阅读,缺少思考的解读,这样的阅读课是低效的,甚至是无效的。因此,如何将阅读课的解读权还给学生、让阅读课堂成为"生本课堂"是本课例探讨的研究问题。

二、教学分析

(一)教材分析

教材选自人教版《普通高中课程标准实验教科书英语必修 4》第一单元。本单元的中心话题是 Women of Achievement,内容包括女性在不同领域获得的非凡成就,她们在获得成就过程中遇到的各种困难以及她们解决困难的经历等。本单元的精读文本记叙了一位研究非洲猩猩的卓越女性 Jane Goodall 的人生经历。通过介绍 Jane，文本表达了女性可以做出男性都很难企及的成就，女性可以克服种种困难同样为世界为人类作出非凡贡献。文章正能量满满，获取简的故事细节是阅读的基本任务，分析 Jane 成功背后的原因是阅读的重心，感受、分享人生启迪是阅读的提升。

从文本信息角度来看，文章共分 4 段，分别介绍了 Jane 研究猩猩的基本方法方式、关于猩猩的研究成果、研究猩猩的目的以及简的成就。虽然每段话仅从一个方面介绍 Jane，是独立的，但是段落间的信息是可以整合的，比如说第一段中的细节 The bond between members of a chimp family is as strong as in human family 既可以认为是关于猩猩的研究成果也可以认为是主人公 Jane 的人生成就；再比如 She spent years observing and recording their daily activities. 虽然在第二段（主要介绍了猩猩的研究成果），但是可以认为是研究方法。文章标题 A Student of African Wildlife 也是文本解读的重要内容之一，通过标题能够预测 who 与 what 的信息，从而布置阅读任务；同时，当学生完成全文阅读后，需要返回标题，辩证思考为什么 Jane 被称为学生。

从文本语言角度来看，文章黑体词涵盖了涉及猩猩行为的词，如 behave、bond、move off 等；涉及 Jane 成就的词，如 inspire, outspoken 等；涉及 Jane 研究方式的词，如 observe 和 behavior 等；涉及 Jane 研究目的的词，如 respect、entertainment、crowd in 和 argue 等。因此，在处理文章信息的过程中，学生就有了理解、分析文章中的生词、重点词的机会。如此，基于文本的语言学习，使词汇的学习不再孤立死板。当然，文章中有语言是学生难以自行解读的，如 Only after her came to help her for the first few months was she allowed to begin her project. 该句除了句子结构复杂难以理解外，更是难以通过解读字面意思明白作者的写作意图；再如，Once I stop, it all comes crowding in and I remember the chimps in laboratories. 该句中，crowd in 是生词，但是上下文却不足以提供足够提示或信息帮助学生自行理解该词组意思；同时 it 的指代模糊，也是学生解读的难点。这些难点成为教学内容，是因为他们不仅承载了文本信息（Jane 虽为女性但却付出常人所不能的努力），还能让学生通过阅读、通过语言学习，获得人生价值体验。

(二) 学生分析

本班大部分学生已经熟练掌握了 scanning、skimming 等阅读技能，他们通过快速阅读获取信息的能力已经得到了很好的训练，这为阅读问题设计提升难度提供了基础。但是学生阅读通常为被动的，即文本解读主要依靠教师的问题引导；他们的阅读是表面化的，即没有反复咀嚼的过程；他们的阅读是模式化的，即阅读是个找信息回答问题的过程。因此，培养学生的批判性阅读能力，教师需要引导学生，更需要给学生充分的机会解读文本并展示自己的解读成果。同时，因为本班学生思维活跃，乐于表达自己的观点，这保证了学生愿意分享自己的解读。当然，在解读过程中，学生仍然会碰到生词理解的问题，遇到归纳、总结的难处,他们的解读需要教师搭建更多有效的"脚手架",帮助他们理解文本,并形成自己特有的解读。

(三) 教学目标

1. 语言能力与学习能力

能使用扫读、跳读等技能快速获得信息,整理归纳 Jane 的研究方法、成果以及目的;能够通过做笔记的方式,把自己对于文本的理解呈现出来,并评价、分享 Jane 的工作以及其为人;充分理解文中的黑体词如 move of、bond、worthwhile、nest、behave、outspoken、argue、crowd in 和 inspire 等,并能在评价环节中使用部分这些词汇;明白文本中 it all comes crowding in 以及 it affects me 中 it 的指代,并通过分析句子补全文中"I will never forget..."后缺少的信息。

2. 文化意识与思维品质

通过阅读,明白女性同样可以在自己的领域做出非凡的成就;通过了解 Jane 的经历,体验为了获得成就需要克服诸多困难,付出常人难以想象的努力。

(四) 教学重点

1. 整理归纳 Jane 研究猩猩的方式、成果、目的以及 Jane 的成就等相关信息;

2. 理解黑体词如 bond、move off、worthwhile、nest、behave、outspoken、argue、crowd in 和 inspire 等在文中的含义并能在评价 Jane 的工作和她的品质中使用部分上述词汇;

3. 根据文章中的信息,整合自己的理解和体验,使用重点词汇与句子,评价 Jane 的工作及其为人,形成自己对于文本的理解。

(五) 教学难点

1. 解读文本中的词汇如 observe、crowd in 和 outspoken 等;解读文本中的语句如 Only after her mother came to help her was she allowed to begin her project.;解读文本中的指代如 it all comes crowding in 中的 it 等;

2. 评价 Jane 的工作与她为人,形成自己特有的文本解读。

(六) 教学思路

本课基于文本解读的层次,采用互动式阅读模式,通过师生互动,教师提供解读方向,学生自主解读文本,使得学生拥有文本解读的主体权;通过学生与文本互动,自行解读文本,阅读出自己的见解,使得学生拥有解读的主动权。本课分为三个阶段。阶段一,语码解读,获取文本信息。通过阅读,了解本文是关于一名普通女性科学家研究猩猩的历程,找到主人公的基本信息(who、what 和 where 等信息)以及她对猩猩的研究成果。阶段二,语用解读,理解文本内容。通过阅读,关注写人的文章中,作者介绍了哪些方面以及作者的写作意图等。阶段三,阐发解读,建构文本意义。通过阅读,研读文字,评价文字背后体现的人物特点,结合自己的解读,评价人物的功绩与性格。

三、 教学实录

一读：语码解读,获取文本信息

问题设计(Designed Questions)

Q1. What do you know about the animals?

Q2. Who is the student?

Q3. What does the animal in the title refer to?

Q4. What else do you want to get from the passage?

课堂情景再现

T： Good morning, everyone! Look at these pictures. What are these animals?

Ss： Chimps.

T： Read after me, chimps.

Ss： Chimps.

T： What do you know about chimps?

S1： They are clever.

T： (Write "clever" on the blackboard)

S2： They are strong. They hunt other animals.

T： (Write "strong" on the blackboard)

S3： They live in trees.

T： (Write "live in trees" on the blackboard)

T： What do we call the place they live in?

S： Nest.

T： (Write the word on the blackboard) Read after me, nest.

Ss： Nest.

T： What else?

S4： They sleep together.

T： (Write "sleep together" on the blackboard) OK, now, I think everyone in the class has known something about these lovely animals. Now, please read the passage and find out whether these things about chimps on the blackboard are mentioned in the passage. You will only be given 2 minutes so read in a "Z" way, focus on the relevant details and underline the information.

Ss: (read the passage)
T: (face the whole class) Clever, mentioned?
Ss: No.
T: Strong?
Ss: No.
T: Sleep in trees?
Ss: Yes.
T: Sleep together?
Ss: Yes.
T: What else do you know from the passage?
S5: They wake up in the morning.
T: How about during the day? What do they do?
S5: They feed or clean each other.
T: Good. How about in the evening? What do they do?
S5: They sleep in the nest.
T: Thank you. What else?
S6: They can communicate.
T: How can they communicate?
S6: They can use their body language.
T: And?
S6: (thinking)
T: Thank you anyway. Anyone? Oh, thank you, please.
S7: They can make a lot of noises.
T: That's a good answer. Take your seat please. Now, everyone, read the title.
Ss: A student of Africa Wildlife.
T: I think we have already known who the student is. Who is he or she?
Ss: She is Jane Goodall.
T: What does she do?
S8: She is a scientist.
T: Who studies … ?
S8: Chimps.
T: Good. Thank you. What does the "African Wildlife" refer to in the passage?
Ss: Chimps.
T: Besides who and what, based on the title, what else do you want to get from the passage?

Ss: (Think for a while)

S9: Why does she study chimps?

T: You?

S10: How does she do the studies?

【设计意图与教学效果】 一读,为的是处理表层信息,明白阅读文本的大意,获取相关文本主干信息。首先,课文的插图能够激活学生的背景知识,同时能够快速导入话题;因为文本内容与图片内容息息相关,因此,学生的背景知识还可以有效地用作读前的预测,可谓一举两得。带着预测阅读问题,寻找相关信息,训练扫读技能,学生能够快速获取文章大意。接着,解读标题,梳理刚刚获得的阅读信息,提出新的阅读问题,为第二遍阅读提供阅读任务。

在此阶段,虽然课堂是按照教师的解读思路进行的,但是,在整个活动中,学生的参与却是积极的、主动的;并且,伴随着学生解读的深入,他们能够自己提出问题,基于问题,自行解读文本。教师在接下来的阅读环节中,只是一个问题设计者、学生解读的评价者、课堂教学的总结者,学生才是文本的解读主体,学生才是文本产生新义的创造者。

一读力求贯穿全文,完成难度较低的阅读任务,如此,能够保证学生保护阅读的积极性,同时保证学生能够总览全文,避免"只见树木不见森林"。本节课,导入加一读用时7分钟,用时短,效率高,同时获得了文章大意,为下面的学生的自主解读铺设了台阶。

二读:语用解读,理解文本内容

问题设计(Designed Questions)

Q1. How does she study the chimps?

Q2. Why does she study the chimps?

Q3. Why does the writer call Jane a student?

Q4. What is the writing purpose?

课堂情景再现

T: Now read the passage and find out answers to the questions. (How does she study the chimps? Why does she study the chimps?) I will give you 3 minutes to finish this activity.

Ss: (Read and think)

T: Would you please tell me how she studies the chimps?

S11: She follows the chimps into the forest.

T: That means she studies in the …

S11: Wild.

T: Good. Or we can say she studies chimps in their own habitat. Read after me, habitat.

Ss: Habitat.

T: How does she study the chimps? What about you?

S12: She spent years observing and recording their daily activities.

T: You are a careful reader. What is the meaning of "observe"?

Ss: 观察.

T: That's right, but how can she observe, can you guess?

S13: Write down something.

T: She can take notes and set them down in her notebook. Right.

S13: (Nodding his head)

T: What else can she do?

S14: She can use a camera.

T: To take photos and videos, right?

S14: Yes.

T: Good. Why does she study the chimps?

S15: Make the world understand and respect the life of these animals.

T: Where can you find the words?

S15: In paragraph 3, line 24.

T: OK, let's read the sentence. One, two, go.

Ss: For forty years Jane Goodall has been outspoken about making the rest of the world understand and respect the life of these animals.

T: What is the meaning of "outspoken"?

Ss: 直言的.

T: Yes, but can you replace the word?

Ss: (Think and feel puzzled)

T: Straightforward, honest, right?

Ss: (Nodding)

T: Now, let's come back to the title. Jane is a scientist, but the writer calls her a student. Why is she called a student? Discuss with your partners.

Ss: (Talk and think)

T: Sorry to stop your discussion. And would you please air your opinion?

S16: She studies the chimps just like we study subjects. So she is a student.

T: En, good. Next.

S17: There are more to study about the chimps. And I think she needs to do more to help the chimps.

T: That's nice. So everybody, we have already known who, what, why and how. Can you tell me the writing purpose of the passage? You can find the hints from the passage or you can discuss with your partners. Now, do it.

Ss: (Read, think and talk)

T: Now, can anyone tell me your idea?

S18: Introduce Jane.

T: What specific information do we know about Jane?

S18: She studies chimps.

T: Why does she study the chimps?

S18: Inspire others who want to succeed.

T: Good. So, put all the answers in one sentence and you will get the purpose.

S18: The purpose of the passage is to introduce Jane and her work, which inspires others who want to succeed.

T: Good job.

【设计意图与教学效果】 二读,为的是探究深层信息,解读写作意图。在一读的基础上,学生自行主动提出阅读任务,探究 how 与 why 的问题。在完成阅读任务的同时,学习、理解、探究文中的黑体词,不仅能够帮助学生理解文本信息,更能学习词汇。在完成全文细节的阅读后,批判性地思考标题,有效地验证学生对全文的理解,巩固前面的阅读活动。最后,学生讨论、探究写作意图,从而加强其概括能力的培养。

在此阶段,学生的阅读处于半开放状态,即学生自主探究阅读文本,独立完成阅读任务。学生的阅读是自由的,时间是充裕的。在此基础上,学生才能透彻理解文本,深入思考,提出自己的质疑,提出自己的见解。

二读,不再是细节上的探究,它是基于一读的基础上的,所以学生的理解应该是深入的。在此过程中,教师不要干预学生的阅读进程,给学生充裕的解读时间,让学生在开放式或半开放式的问题的引导下,提出自己的阅读任务,反思自己的阅读结果,质疑文本中的阅读细节。本课中,学生在回答问题时言之有理,思考深入,很好地做到了"知其然而知其所以然"。

三读:阐发解读,建构文本意义

问题设计(Designed Questions)

Q1. What do you think of Jane?

Q2. What do you think of her work?

Q3. What does "it" refer to?

Q4. What does "that" refer to?

Q5. What can be possibly continued after "you can never forget …"?

课堂情景再现

T: Jane, who is a woman, has achieved so much in her career. But is her work easy to do?

Ss: No.

T: Now, read the passage for the third time. Think about what kind of person Jane is.

	Then what do you think of her work? After reading, organize your idea in the following way. (PPT: The work is _____ because _____. So as far as I am concerned, she is a person who is _____.)
Ss:	(Read and think)
T:	Now, can you tell me your answer?
S19:	The work is hard because they have to go back to the place where they left the family sleep. So as far as I am concerned, she is a person who is hard-working.
T:	I like your answer. You?
S20:	The work is challenging because only after her mother came to help her for the first few months was she allowed to begin her project. So as far as I am concerned, she is brave.
T:	The idea is brilliant. You've done a good job. How about you?
S21:	The work is meaningful because she has argued that the wild animals should be left in the wild and not used for entertainment or advertisement. As far as I am concerned, she is a person who is devoted to her work and who loves animals.
T:	So that is why she can inspire others. Speaking of kindness, I have found something in the passage. Please read it first.
Ss:	"Once I stop, it all comes crowding in and I remember the chimps in the laboratories. It's terrible. It affects me when I watch the wild chimps, I say to myself, 'Aren't they lucky?' And then I think about small chimps in cages though they have done nothing wrong. Once you have seen that you can never forget..."
T:	What does "it" in "it all comes crowding in" refer to?
S22:	Chimps suffer because of human.
T:	Can you get an example from the passage?
S22:	The chimps in the laboratories. Small chimps in cages.
T:	Good. Aren't they lucky? Who are lucky? Why are they lucky?
S23:	Wild chimps. They are lucky because they are in the wild, away from human.
T:	That's right. So in the sentence, "once you have seen that", what does "that" refer to?
S24:	Small chimps in cages.
T:	Good. So when Jane sees chimps in the wild, she feels happy. However, seeing chimps in cages, she feels sad. So what can be continued after "you can never forget..."? Think, discuss in groups and give me at least three sentences.
Ss:	(Read, think and talk)
T:	Who'd like to be the first one? Thank you, please.
S25:	Once you have seen that you can never forget the sufferings of the chimps. You can

find them sad in the cages. You know you can do more to help the chimps.

T: That's good. What about you?

S26: Once you have seen that you can never forget the tears in the chimps' eyes. You can never forget that humans are cruel to the animals. And you can never forget there are a lot left for us to do to protect these lovely animals.

T: Wow, what do you think of her answer?

S27: Very good. Her answer is related to the passage. She uses "排比". She describes a lot.

T: Nice. She uses good words including using parallelism and her description is vivid.

【设计意图与教学效果】 三读,为的是鉴赏语言,品读作者的语言风格,品味阅读的德育价值。在前两读的基础上,学生通过三读,评价Jane的工作和她的为人。这是一篇写人的文章,因此,文中有多处语言表现人物性格、品质的评价。这是该类文本的共同之处。因此,学生能够依据文本有话可讲,有情可抒。当然,作为语言的课堂,学习语言、解决语言造成的阅读难点理应成为课堂教学的重要环节。因此,在课堂的最后阶段,提出难点、解决难点也是学生所需。

在此阶段,学生对文本进行更为深入的解读,利用从本文获取的信息,使用文本中的语言,发表自己的见解,分享各自的解读。这一阶段,学生的思想与原作者的思想交流,此时的文本阅读,基于文本而又超越文本。

三读,是基于全文的良好理解下的阅读。这一阶段的阅读,是对文本语言的欣赏、是对文本情感价值的体验、是对文化内涵的升华,同时也是解决文本中因为语言、文化带来的阅读难点的关键。此时的阅读,是统领全文的阅读,是自由的阅读,更是批判的、反思的阅读。但不管读什么,阅读仍然要基于文本的语言,基于文本的信息。本课中,学生的评价是精彩的、独到的,学生对难点解读有条理、有层次,如此的阅读,层次分明、难度适中、落实全面。

四、 教学反思

(一) 合理设置任务难度,给学生留下充分解读的时间

通过课堂观察,我们不难发现,有的教师课堂教学推进很慢,学生的回答往往不尽人意,究其原因还是教师设置的阅读任务难度过高,导致学生的解读受阻,同时教师又没有给学生留出充裕的时间,教学活动的推进往往只重其表,而不重其实。因此,教师应该设计难度合理的阅读任务。本节课,教师设置了难度不大的一读任务,学生只需要根据阅读问题,在文中找到相应的内容即可。问题难度稍大的第二读,是基于文本内容的总结概括,只要能够言之有理,在文本中找寻证据即可完成,同时教师给了学生更多的时间,保证了这一步骤的顺利进行。难度最大的第三读,基于全文理解的基础上,学生对于文本有了自己的认识与理解,因此,产出结果质量较高。从本节课看,要想学生能充分地解读文本,得出质量较高的解读成果,需要设计适合学生层次的教学活动。这里所谓的"适合",不仅仅是难度上适合,更是教师的解读视角不能凌驾于学生理解之上,即阅读活动要么能够机械地从文本上获得

答案,要么能够灵活地从文本中获得信息解决问题,不要设计既不能从文本中得到答案,又不能根据文本合理推测的问题。在设计活动难度的同时,课堂给学生完成任务的时间要充裕,如此才能保证学生全面、细致地解读文本。

(二) 巧妙设计问题类型,给学生搭建逐步解读的支架

阅读问题通常有三种类型：展示型问题、参考型问题和评估型问题,三种问题类型的开放程度由小到大递增,培养的思辨能力也属不同层次。英语阅读课上,有的教师重信息整理,轻人物评价,学生的高层次思辨能力得不到培养；有的教师则重人物评价,轻信息整理,学生思辨能力的培养就没有一个稳定的支架。本堂课三个阅读环节的问题类型不同。"一读"重在教师引导,阅读问题属于封闭式的展示型问题,学生只要找到答案即可；"二读"重在学生归纳和推断,阅读问题属于半开放式的参考型问题,学生不仅要能找到信息,还要对信息进行提炼加工；"三读"重在提升,阅读问题主要属于开放式的评估型问题,另外"三读"还涉及了对文中重难点的突破和理解。三个阅读环节不同类型的问题培养学生不同层次的思辨能力。在"一读"中,学生要做的是搜索信息和预测,属于较低层次思维的训练；"二读"中,学生要分析和推断,属于较高层次的思维训练；"三读"中学生要评价创造,属于高层次的思维训练。在三个阅读环节中,问题的思维层次逐渐从低层次过渡到高层次,学生的思维能力也逐渐从低层次向高层次发展。这样的设计避免了学生直接面临高级思维问题的困难,让学生的思维有一个缓冲、适应、提升的过程,逐步提高学生思维的参与程度,为学生搭建了一个解读文本的支架。

(三) 关注师生互动模式,给学生留出自行解读的机会

学生没有解读的机会,那是因为教师把学生解读的机会都占了。教师成为课堂的"劳动者",事必躬亲,将阅读问题精心设计,将学生的回答精心预设。这样的课堂上,学生是附属的,他们的任务只是执行教师的教学设计,走完了教师事先铺好的路。这样的课堂,要么"死气沉沉"——学生的思维跟不上教师的,学生解读深度跟不上教师；要么"一团和气"——学生无需思考,他们只要完成教师环环相扣的任务即可。不管是哪种课堂,课堂还是教师的,学生只是配合着,课堂没有惊喜、没有生成。因此,要给学生留出解读的机会,要让他们主动地参与到文本解读中来,养成习惯,形成技能。本节课中,在不同的阅读阶段,教师与学生互动的模式因不同类型、不同难度的文本解读问题而有所不同。"一读"过程中,教师的角色比较重要,把握文本的解读方向,布置阅读任务,提出阅读问题,学生的学习是在教师的指导下完成的；"二读"时,学生已经能够自主整理信息,对文本内容适当推断；"三读"时,学生已有个人观点的表达、有创造性的思维成果。后两遍阅读中,学生的解读越来越多,教师在教学过程中只是监听者和评价者。整个阅读课堂教师慢慢放手,学生逐渐独立、顺利地完成了文本解读任务。

(课例撰写：温州第二中学　项纸陆　浙江师范大学　杨聪聪)

教材文本

A STUDENT OF AFRICAN WILDLIFE

It is 5:45 am and the sun is just rising over Gombe National Park in East Africa. Following Jane's way of studying chimps, our group are all going to visit them in the forest. Jane has studied these families of chimps for many years and helped people understand how much they behave like humans. Watching a family of chimps wake up is our first activity of the day. This means going back to the place where we left the family sleeping in a tree the night before. Everybody sits and waits in the shade of the trees while the family begins to wake up and move off. Then we follow as they wander into the forest. Most of the time, chimps either feed or clean each other as a way of showing love in their family. Jane warns us that our group is going to be very tired and dirty by the afternoon and she is right. However, the evening makes it all worthwhile. We watch the mother chimp and her babies play in the tree. Then we see them go to sleep together in their nest for the night. We realize that the bond between members of a chimp family is as strong as in a human family.

Nobody before Jane fully understood chimp behaviour. She spent years observing and recording their daily activities. Since her childhood she had wanted to work with animals in their own environment. However, this was not easy. When she first arrived in Gombe in 1960, it was unusual for a woman to live in the forest. Only after her mother came to help her for the first few months was she allowed to begin her project. Her work changed the way people think about chimps. For example, one important thing she discovered was that chimps hunt and eat meat. Until then everyone had thought chimps ate only fruit and nuts. She actually observed chimps as a group hunting a monkey and then eating it. She also discovered how chimps communicate with each other, and her study of their body language helped her work out their social system.

For forty years Jane Goodall has been outspoken about making the rest of the world understand and respect the life of these animals. She has argued that wild animals should be left in the wild and not used for entertainment or advertisements. She has helped to set up special places where they can live safely. She is leading a busy life but she says: "Once I stop, it all comes crowding in and I remember the chimps in laboratories. It's terrible. It affects me when I watch the wild chimps. I say to myself, 'Aren't they lucky?' And then I think about small chimps in cages though they have done nothing wrong. Once you have seen that you can never forget ..."

　　She has achieved everything she wanted to do: working with animals in their own environment, gaining a doctor's degree and showing that women can live in the forest as men can. She inspires those who want to cheer the achievements of women.

说课案例九（词汇课）

PEP M3U3 The Million Pound Bank Note

　　各位老师大家好，非常高兴有机会开设一节词汇课，与各位老师共同探讨高中英语词汇教学的有效途径。一直以来，一线教师一直没有停止对高中英语词汇有效教学的探索。因为我们重视词汇，词汇是语言之基，因为Without vocabulary, nothing can be conveyed。然而，在以技能为本的高中英语教学中，我们探索词汇课有效教学途径的时候存在诸多困惑。困惑一是如何正确处理词汇教学与阅读教学的关系。相对独立的词汇课是作为单元第一课时在阅读课前开设，还是作为第二课时在阅读课之后开设？作为阅读课前第一课时的词汇课，教师在设计词汇课时往往脱离阅读文本语境而又不另行创设语境，耗时又低效。作为阅读课后第二课时的词汇课，如果不加处理沿用阅读文本语境，又难以避免"炒冷饭"的低效重复。困惑二是如何选择词汇教学内容。词汇教学内容庞杂，既要关注词汇的语境意义与文化内涵，又要关注词汇的习惯用法与固定搭配；既要关注词句单位的词汇学习和操练，又要关注语篇单位的词汇运用，如此繁重的任务加重了学生的学习负担，也给教师备课带来诸多麻烦。一堂令人满意的词汇课需要教师创设适合目标词汇的教学情境，需要教师去构建涵盖目标词汇的语句与篇章，需要编写针对性的课后练习等。那么，如何充分利用阅读语篇，减少师生"巨大的"付出和投入，基于语篇重构，开展词汇教学，保证教学效果已成为高中英语教学研究的重要关切，也是本节课的研讨目标。

一、教学目标定位

　　本节课的文本标题是 The Million Pound Bank Note，选自人教版高中英语必修三第三单元，是开设在第二课时的词汇课，目标词汇有 bet、survive、stare at、penniless、wander、nightfall 和 spot 等。本课的目标词汇众多，并且多数粗体词需要情境支持方能确定词汇的含义与用法。不同的目标词汇对学生能力的要求不同，有些词汇只需掌握其音形义即可，有些词汇则需要归纳、总结它的用法，有些词汇需要在情境中运用等。此外，由于目标词汇之间话题与语义的相关度较小，脱离原文本语境再创设涵盖所有目标词汇的情境难度较大，重构原阅读语篇也有一定难度。

在研读文本的基础上,我将文本脉络重新梳理成"一个赌约"、"一场海难"和"一张钞票",分别对应黑板上紫色、蓝色和黄色的部分。"一个赌约"是指 Oliver 兄弟打赌持有一张百万英镑是否能够在英国生活一个月。"一场海难"描述的是 Henry 只身一人来到英国的奇遇。"一张钞票"是指 Oliver 兄弟遇到 Henry,了解 Henry 之后交给他一张百万英镑。依据以上对文章脉络和教学情境的重组,我将本节课划分为三个教学环节。每个环节都涉及不同词汇的学习和操练,所有的目标词汇都涵盖在本单元阅读情境下,词与词之间有了联系。有了情境的依托,词汇的单项训练就容易设计。

基于以上的教材分析,本堂课共有 3 个语言知识与语言技能目标。首先,学生要通过对课内和课外例句的归纳,整理出 bet 作为名词和动词的用法,并在真实语境中使用;第二,通过 Henry 来到英国的经历,在语篇中掌握 nightfall、spot、passage、embassy 和 seek 等目标词汇;第三,通过学生对文本的理解以及所给词组,paraphrase 文中句子,推测 Henry 情绪的变化,通过复述全文,深化阅读理解。

二、教学目标达成

从教学效果看,本课的教学目标设置合理,体现了词汇学习不同层面的要求。这里我会具体说明一下本节课的教学目标是如何通过相应的教学活动一一达成的。

首先,在导入环节,我呈现了一张泰坦尼克号剧照,要求学生联想单词 scene 的相关词汇。紧接着借着"场景"一词,我呈现一张过年背景下流浪汉的图片,要求学生根据流浪汉的神情,使用目标词汇描述图片。从课堂效果看,学生能够准确使用 stare at 和 penniless 等目标词汇,正确使用 as if 句型创造性地描述图片,新旧知识得以完美结合。导入环节结合特定情境,呈现和操练了目标词汇,词汇学习从词到短语再到句子,联想记忆,层层递进,学习效果好。

承接导入环节,我设计了一个找词造句的活动。流浪汉看到了一串字谜,要求学生从这些字母中,按排列顺序找出相关单词,并要求学生基于文本的理解用找出的词汇造句(The two brothers made a bet if Henry could survive a month in London with a million pound bank note.)。教师简要讲解后呈现涵盖 bet 作为名词和动词用法的例句,要求学生模仿造句。这一环节中,bet 作为本课的重点词汇,得到了充分的重视。通过对课内外例句的整理与归纳,学生能够在真实的情境中复习和活用 bet 作为名词和动词的各种用法,教学目标一得以达成。还有本节课的找词造句活动,也大大激发了学生课堂参与的积极性,保证了目标词汇的有效学习。

教学目标二是要求学生能够根据关键词,按时间顺序复述 Henry 只身来到英国的经历。首先,要求学生回忆当 Oliver 兄弟在遇到 Henry 时的情境。学生使用目标词汇说出"At this moment, they saw a penniless young man wandering on the pavement"。学生在理解 penniless 与 wandering 的含义之后,再用自己的语言解释该句。然后我再要求学生在理解文本的基础上,去回顾 Henry 只身来到英国的经过。我向学生提供故事的时间、地点和事件等关键词,先要求全班一起复述故事,然后撤去黑板上关于时间与地点的关键词,要求个别学生复述故事。最后,撤去所有的关键词,再让全班一起复述故事。四次复述,不是简单的死记硬背,而是通过可用关键词的不断减少,不断增加任务难度,学生从对目标词汇的简单运用,到基于对文本的理解创造性地使用目标词汇,大大地提高了学生课堂的参与程度和积极性,取得了良好的教学效果。

教学目标三是提高学生基于理解的 paraphrase 技能和复述技能。首先我要求学生基于文本的理解,选用所给的词条 paraphrase 文中的几个例句:1. I landed in Britain by accident. 2. It was all my fault. I'd just about given myself up when I was spotted by a ship. 3. I earned my passage by working as an unpaid hand, which accounts for my appearance. 这个环节的 paraphrase,不是机械地使用近义词、同义词完成练习,而是学生灵活地重述自己对故事的理解。在这个环节中,学生的 paraphrase 技能得到初步训练。

因为作为第一课时阅读课上只解决了故事的梗概和人物性格分析,因此,在本堂课上,我带领学生从词汇层面分析人物的话语从而兼顾对文本的深层解读。首先,我要求学生通读全文,找寻描写 Henry 情绪变化的词句。通过本活动,学生体验了表示礼貌、生气、困惑等多种情绪的表达方式和表达效果,欣赏性阅读目标达成。接着我要求学生在无词条辅助的情况下,去 paraphrase 文中表示人物情绪的几个例句。这个环节的 paraphrase 相比上一个环节来说难度更大,学生 paraphrase 的技能得到进一步的提升。接着我又通过三个问题为学生搭建复述全文的支架,1. How did Henry come to England? 2. How did he meet the brothers? 3. What happened between them? 学生在回答三个问题的基础上,对全文进行了复述。相比上一个"海难"环节的复述,最后环节的任务涵盖的信息量更大,学生需要根据自己对文本的理解,在思维导图的帮助下灵活运用所有的目标词汇。但因为上面几个环节的稳扎稳打,这个环节的任务虽然难度较大,抛去个别语法错误来说,学生也顺利地完成了任务。

三、教学得失反思

本堂研讨课旨在探讨高中英语词汇教学的有效方法。从教学效果看,本堂课有三个有效的教学实践:1. 充分利用阅读文本,重构词汇教学语境;2. 明确词汇学习的分层目标,实施目标词汇的分层教学;3. 巧妙运用思维导图,搭建词汇学习网络。

(一) 充分利用阅读文本,重构词汇教学语境

词汇教学与阅读教学相结合是高中英语词汇教学的重要途径。单元目标词汇往往集中在阅读文本中,而阅读文本本身就是一个理想的话题情境。因此充分利用教材、深入挖掘文本,不仅可以给词汇课提供充足的语言素材和话题情境,也可以减少教师在寻找合适话题时的负担。另外,高中英语教材的阅读文本普遍偏长,生词偏多,发展学生高层次阅读理解技能的任务逐渐加重,因此一个课时的阅读课很难兼顾语言学习和深层理解。阅读文本的再

次使用，能够加深学生对于该情境下目标词汇的理解，也使繁重的学习任务化整为零，保护了学生持续学习的热情。因此，教师有必要重新梳理文本脉络，重组阅读语篇，重构词汇语境，在阅读语境下呈现、操练和运用目标词汇，通过 Paraphrase、Retelling 和 Discussing 等活动进一步加深学生对阅读文本深层寓意的产出性理解。从我们的教学实践来看，基于阅读文本语境，以词汇学习和运用为主要目标的语篇层次的词汇教学尝试是有益的、有效的。学生的词汇学习有个接触、理解、记忆、运用、巩固的渐进过程，学习效果是有保障的。

（二）明确词汇学习的分层目标，实施目标词汇的分层教学

高中英语倡导学生通过语篇阅读理解词汇在语境中的含义。因此，不管一个单元的目标词汇有多少个，多数生词会首次出现在阅读文本中。但是作为第一课时的阅读课如果过度关注生词，就会影响阅读技能的培养。因此，教师应该实现词汇的分层教学。作为第一课时的阅读，教师应该去关注生词在语境中的意义理解，关注那些用法和搭配会影响阅读理解的生词，适当讲解以帮助学生在语用层面上解读文本。总而言之，第一课时中的词汇教学主要关注词汇在语境中的含义，是属于语篇单位的词汇教学。作为侧重词汇教学的阅读课第二课时，教师备课的首要任务就是筛选和整理出本科的重点词汇，明确哪些词汇需要掌握其音形义，哪些词汇需要归纳其用法，哪些词汇需要在语境中呈现、操练和运用。因此，作为第二课时的词汇课既有语句层面的词汇教学，也有语篇层面的词汇教学。总之，教师需要明确词汇学习的分层目标，发展学生重点词汇的语用能力。词句单位的词汇教学更多关注词法和句法，而语篇单位的词汇教学关注重点词汇在语境中的灵活运用。

（三）巧妙运用思维导图，搭建词汇学习网络

如何有效识记单词应该是一直以来困扰学生的一大难题，而思维导图作为一种显性的思维工具和学习方法，可以促进学生对词汇的理解和识记。

教师往往会通过板书来呈现新词，然而传统的板书只能顾及词汇的拼写，往往会忽略单词的词性、意义和用法，而思维导图则可以让学生通过词语词之间的联系去推测词性、意义和用法，使词汇内部的知识外显出来，学生对单词的理解也更具逻辑性。同时思维导图对词汇的识记也大有助益，学生可以通过思维导图来回顾所学词汇，使思维过程和记忆方法有迹可循，加深了记忆的痕迹，增强了记忆的效果。因此英语教师可以巧妙地运用思维导图，促进学生对词汇的理解，攻克单词"难记易忘"的难题。

总之，选用阅读情境和巧用思维导图，可以建立词汇之间的联系，可以发散词汇的学习内容，可以减轻教师词汇课备课负担，以上就是我对本堂课的教学反思。当然本堂课仍然存在一些不足之处，还请各位老师批评指正。

（说课稿撰写：温州第二中学　项纸陆　浙江师范大学　杨聪聪）

附：教学课例及教材文本

PEP NSEFC M3 U3 The Million Pound Bank Note

一、课例背景

一直以来，一线教师从未停止探索词汇教学有效途径。教师重视词汇，因为词汇是语言之基（Without vocabulary, nothing can be conveyed）。然而，在以技能为本的高中英语教学中，我们探索词汇课有效教学时存在诸多困惑。困惑一是如何正确处理词汇教学与阅读教学的关系。相对独立的词汇课是安排在单元第一课时，即在阅读课前开设，还是作为第二课时在阅读课之后开设？作为第一课时的词汇课，教师在设计词汇课时往往脱离阅读文本语境而又不另行创设语境，词汇学习常常脱离语境，耗时却低效。作为阅读课后第二课时的词汇课，如果不加处理沿用阅读文本语境，就又脱不开"炒冷饭"的低效重复。困惑二是如何选择词汇教学内容。词汇教学内容庞杂，既要关注词汇的语境意义与文化内涵，又要关注词汇的习惯用法与固定搭配；既要关注词句单位的词汇学习和操练，又要关注词汇语篇单位的运用。如此繁重的学习内容，不但加重了学生的学习负担，也给教师备课带来诸多麻烦：一堂满意的词汇课需要教师创设适合目标词汇的教学情境，需要构建涵盖目标词汇的语句与篇章，需要编写课后针对性练习等。那么，如何充分利用阅读语篇，减少师生"巨大的"投入，基于语篇重构，开展词汇教学，保证教学效果已成为高中英语教学研究的重要关注点，也是本节课的研讨目标。

二、教学分析

（一）教材分析

本节词汇课教材选自人教版普通高中课程标准实验教科书英语必修3第3单元，目标词汇有 survive、wander、permit、spot、seek、bet、penniless、passage、embassy、nightfall、bay、by accident、go ahead、stare at、on the contrary、account for 和 in rags 等。本课的目标词汇多，多数黑体词需要情境支持方能确定词汇的含义与用法，不同的目标词汇要求学生能力的参与程度是不同，有的只需了解音、形、义，有的则需要总结用法，有的需要在情境中运用等。此外，由于目标词汇之间话题与语义的相关度较小，脱离原文本语境再创设涵盖所有目标词汇的合适的情境难度较大。因此，使用原阅读文本，构建词汇教学框架显得顺理成章。

阅读文章是一剧本，改编自美国作家马克•吐温创作的中篇小说《百万英镑》。原文这一幕讲述 Oliver 和 Roderick 兄弟俩碰到流落到英国的落魄青年 Henry，打赌拥有百万英镑的他是饿死还是过得很好。文章的脉络可以梳理成"一个赌约、一场海难和一张钞票"。一个赌约是指 Oliver 兄弟打赌持有百万英镑是否能够在英国生活一个月。一场海难是指 Henry 无意间来到英国的奇遇。一张钞票是指 Oliver 兄弟了解 Henry 情况后交给他的百万英镑。利用文本脉络可以涵盖绝大部分目标词汇，但是仍然有部分词汇无法整合。另外，文章情境只能提供词汇一个语境，部分词汇一词多义，因此，需要教师在原有情境上再增设例句，创设情境。

（二）学生分析

本课是本单元的第二课时，基于阅读第一课时，学生已经获取了故事的梗概与细节，知道谁做了什么事情；基于细节，推测了人物的性格；基于文本内容，思考了作者的写作意图。而实现上述目标，需要学生能够读懂文字，知道阅读中语句的字面意思，因此，本节词汇课的教学是基于学生已经掌握了阅读文本语境下的目标词汇的含义，换句话说，学生已经掌握了词汇的某一含义，达到了辨识的程度。但是，从知道到运用，学生还需要更多的学习机会和指导。另外，部分词汇如 scene、spot 和 passage 等词需要学生掌握更多的含义。对于词汇学习，历来是学生学习的难点，他们多学却少用，多翻译却少表达，多识记却少推敲；他们学习方法单一，以至于学习效率不高；他们使用词汇可能是词单位的，可能是句单位的，少篇章单位的。课堂教学中，由于词汇教学往往枯燥单调，学生缺少学习的兴趣。因此，丰富多样的词汇学习活动是有效词汇课的重要保证。

（三）教学目标

1. 能根据课内和课外的例句，归纳 bet 的词汇用法，并在真实语境中使用；
2. 通过复述 Henry 来到英国的经历，在语篇中复习和活用如 passage、unpaid hand 和 bay 等目标词汇；
3. 结合文本情境，用自己的语言 paraphrase 文中的例句，推测 Henry 的情绪，通过复述全文，加深阅读理解。

（四）教学重点

通过具体词汇学习，熟练使用 paraphrasing；通过使用关键词和逻辑连接词，复述文章故事。

（五）教学难点

熟练使用多种词汇学习方法学习并使用词汇，如 paraphrasing、grouping 和 associating 等；使用表示时间关系的逻辑连接词复述文章故事。

（六）教学思路

本课将利用文本脉络（一个赌约、一场海难和一张钞票），基于原文故事，创设情境，依据

3P教学模式,设置五步教学环节。首先,利用图片导入,描述图片,使用目标词汇(penniless 和 stare at 等);再结合图片,引出并学习 bet,然后链接课文;依据文章脉络,利用"打赌"情境,完成 bet 和 survive 的呈现和操练;在"故事"环节,完成 wander、penniless、nightfall、spot、passage、embassy 和 seek 等词汇的学习;利用"钞票"情境,完成 on the contrary 和 go ahead 等词汇学习,推敲说话者的情绪变化;在完成所有词汇的学习和操练后,转述故事,巩固所有本课所学词汇。本课将词汇学习主要分散在三个不同的情境片段中,通过模仿造句、根据关键词复述故事、用自己的话解释文本原句、品读文本理解词汇的表情达意等活动,展开词汇的学习与运用。

三、教学实录

步骤一:图片导入,链接文章

Enjoy the two pictures, recall relevant words and talk.

T: Morning, everyone. To start with, I'd like to show two pictures. What does this picture remind you of?

Ss: Titanic.

T: That's right. Then what does Titanic remind you of?

S1: Movie.

S2: Sadness.

T: Yes. Titanic reminds us of shocking scenes. Read after me. Scene. Scene.

Ss: Scene. Scene.

T: What does this word mean?

Ss: 一幕,场景。

T: Yes. So Titanic reminds you of what scenes?

S3: Titanic reminds me of sad scenes.

S4: Titanic reminds me of terrifying scenes as there were thousands of people falling into icy water.

T: You've done an amazing job. What about you?

S5: Titanic reminds me of romantic scenes where Jack held Rose from the back.

T: Terrific. Then, what about this picture? What does it remind you of?

S6: A poor man.

S7: A beggar.

T: Yes, he is a tramp. What words does this tramp remind you of?

S8: Poor, penniless.

S9: He stared at the sky as if wondering what to do for his Spring Festival.

T: Good sentence, thank you. Of course, it can remind you of a lot of words. One day, the tramps saw a puzzle. Can you pick out words from the 28 letters? (VWBETCANSURVIVENOTEMONTHIFEF)?

【设计意图与教学效果】 使用泰坦尼克号剧照,要求学生根据图片联想单词 scene 的相关词汇,比如 a sad scene 和 a terrifying scene。学生在语境中透彻理解 scene 的含义。紧接着借着"场景"一词,我呈现以过年为背景的一个流浪汉的图片(图中流浪汉面带微笑,仰天凝视),要求学生根据流浪汉的神情描述图片,使用目标词汇(penniless、stare at、wander、seek 和 in rags)。从课堂效果看,学生能够充分运用联想记忆这一词汇学习策略,准确使用 penniless 等目标词汇,正确使用 as if 句型等创造性地描述图片,新旧知识得以完美结合。导入环节结合特定语境,呈现和操练了目标词汇,词汇学习从词到短语再到句子,联想记忆,层层递进,学习效果好。

步骤二:识辨词汇,模仿造句

Pick out words from letters arranged in a random way. Focus on the word BET. Study the sentences, summarize the usage of BET and make sentences by imitating.

T: Can you pick out some words from these letters-VWBETCANSURVIVENOTEMO-NTHILLIFV?

Ss: (bet/a/can/survive/note/month/if)

T: Can you recall the bet Oliver and Rodrick made on Henry? What is it? The two brothers made …

Ss: The two brothers made a bet whether Henry could survive a month in London with a million pound bank note.

T: What is a note?

Ss: Money.

T: Yes. Study the two sentences and pay attention to how to use bet. (I bet that it will rain tomorrow. Have you ever made a bet with a friend?)

T: What are the parts of speech of bet in these two sentences?

Ss: Noun and verb.

T: Have you ever made a bet with someone? What was the bet?

S10: I made a bet with my father that if I could get 100 in exam, he would buy me a bike.

S11: I bet our team could win in the school basketball game.

T: You all have done a good job.

【设计意图与教学效果】 承接导入环节,创设情境,要求学生从 28 个字母中,按排列顺序找出六个单词 bet、can、survive、one、note 和 month,然后结合阅读文章用找出的词汇造句 The two brothers made a bet whether Henry could survive a month in London with a million pound bank note.。教师简要讲解后呈现涵盖 bet 作为名词和动词用法的例句,要求学生模仿造句。这一环节中,bet 一词作为本课的重点词汇,得到了充分的重视。学生根据例句总结 bet 的用法,并能模仿造句,表达个人观点。本环节找单词活动的设置,充分激发了学生课堂参与的积极性,保证了目标词汇的有效学习。

步骤三:挑战记忆,复述故事

According to the story, recall how Henry came to England by accident. Retell this part of story for three times. For each time, different requirements are set to make this retelling task challenging.

T: So when the two brothers first met Henry and made the bet, what did Henry look like?

Ss: At this moment, they saw a penniless young man wandering on the pavement.

T: Can you paraphrase?

S12: At that time, they saw a young man who was poor without any money and was walking on the street without any purpose.

T: Why was Henry wandering on the pavement?

Ss: He came to London by accident.

T: So do you still remember how Henry landed in London by accident? Now I have picked out words for time and verbs for events. Please put them together and retell the story. First, let's do it together.

T & Ss: About one month ago, Henry was sailing out of the bay. Towards nightfall, he found himself carried out to sea by a strong wind. The next morning, he was about to give up when he was spotted by a ship. During the journey, he earned his passage by working as an unpaid hand. After landing in England, he went to the America embassy for help, but no one helped him.

T: Would you please have a try?

S13: About one month ago, Henry was sailing out of the bay. Towards nightfall, he found himself carried out to sea by a strong wind. The next morning, he was about to give up when he was spotted by a ship. During the journey, he earned his passage by working as an unpaid hand. After landing in England, he went to the America embassy for help, but no one helped him.

T: You've got a good memory. Now, I will cover the words for time, can you do it as well as before? How about you?

S14: About one month ago, Henry was sailing out of the bay. Towards nightfall, he found himself carried out to sea by a strong wind. The next morning, he was about to give up when he was spotted by a ship. During the journey, he earned his passage by working as an unpaid hand. After landing in England, he went to the America embassy for help, but no one helped him.

T: Good. How about covering all the words for events? Please challenge yourself.

S15: About one month ago, Henry was sailing out of the bay. Towards nightfall, he found himself carried out to sea by a strong wind. The next morning, he was about to give up when he was spotted by a ship. During the journey, he earned his passage by working as an unpaid hand. After landing in England, he went to the America embassy for help, but no one helped him.

T: You are amazing. Now, how about retelling the story without any reference? Let's do it together.

Ss: About one month ago, Henry was sailing out of the bay. Towards nightfall, he found himself carried out to sea by a strong wind. The next morning, he was about to give up when he was spotted by a ship. During the journey, he earned his passage by working as an unpaid hand. After landing in England, he went to the America embassy for help, but no one helped him.

T: You amazed me. Now can you paraphrase the sentences taken from the story?

1. I landed in Britain by accident.
2. It was all my fault. I'd just about given myself up when I was spotted by a ship.
3. I earned my passage by working as an unpaid hand, which accounts for my appearance.

You can use the reference words and expressions sin the following box.

(be responsible for; explain; find sth./sb. suddenly; stop trying; by chance; ticket; without payment; the moment; come to)

S16: I came to Britain by chance.

S17: I am responsible for this accident.

S18: I was about to stop trying when I was found by a ship.

S19: I earned my ticket without payment.

S20: This explained my appearance.

T: Good job, everybody.

【设计意图与教学效果】 该步骤的教学目标是学生能够根据关键词,使用时间顺序复述故事;能够基于理解提高 paraphrase 的能力。这里的故事就是 Henry 如何只身来到英国。首先,回忆当 Oliver 兄弟两看到 Henry 的时候,Henry 在做什么,承接上一活动。学生使用目标词汇说出了 At this moment, they saw a penniless young man wandering on the pavement. 然后,要求学生理解 penniless 与 wandering 的含义并用自己的语言解释该句。基于理解,回顾 Henry 无意间来到英国的经过。教师提供故事的时间、地点和事件(主要是动词)等关键词,先要求全班根据关键词一起复述故事,然后遮去课件上关于时间的关键词,要求个别学生复述故事。再接着遮去关于事件的关键词,要求学生根据时间再次复述故事。最后,遮去所有的关键词,要求全班讲述故事。四次复述,并非简单的死记硬背,而是通过不断减少可用关键词,不断增加难度,由简单使用目标词汇,到基于理解创造性地使用目标词汇,循序渐进,大大地提高了学生的积极性与参与度,取得了良好的教学效果。接着,结合故事情节,解释三个句子,不仅仅保证学生更为熟练地使用近义词、同义词,训练 paraphrase 技能,更可以检测学生对于语句和情节的理解。

步骤四:解释原句,品读情绪

Read the passage, infer how Henry felt and find the evidence. Then paraphrase the sentences from the book with their own words.

T: After Henry met the two brothers, a letter was given, during which time Henry's feelings were changing. What were Henry's feelings and how do you know?

S21: Henry was polite. He said, "Go right ahead."

S22: He was confused. He said, "For me?"

S23: He was angry. He said, "On the contrary, in fact. If this is your idea of some kind of joke, I don't think it's very funny."

S24: He was determined. He said, "I just want an honest job."

S25: He was puzzled. He said, "I'm afraid I don't quite follow you, sir."

T: Good. Now, study these sentences you have found from the book. (1. Go right ahead. 2. On the contrary, in fact. 3. I'm afraid I don't quite follow you, sir.) Can you paraphrase?

S26: Please ask.

S27: We are quite different. You are rich, and I am not.

S28: I'm afraid I don't understand you, sir.

T: Good.

【设计意图与教学效果】 该教学步骤再一次训练学生 paraphrase 的技能。上一环节中,学生使用同义词或近义词即可替换原句的关键词,鲜有涉及句型的改变。该环节中的句子需要学生首先理解对词汇的基本含义,然后结合文章情节,使用文章内容解释目标词汇。因此,虽然这仅仅是一个技能,本节课却呈现了多角度、多方法的训练,突出了教学重点。另外,由于第一节课已经完成了全文故事的理解,学生能够在第二课时重点关注语言以及语言背后的情感表现,如此,分散了词汇教学内容,有的放矢,收到了很好的教学效果。

步骤五:转述故事,巩固所学

Retell the whole passage in the third person with answers to reference questions.

T: Now, let's see whether you can use all the words in the passage and tell us a story about how a young man came to London and got a million pound bank note. First you should get the answers to the three questions (1. How did he come to London? 2. How did he meet the two brothers? 3. What happened between the two brothers and Henry?), then you can do the retelling. I have given you the start. Now, do it by yourself and then we will share your story.

Ss: (Prepare the retelling)

T: Can you have a try?

S29: This story is an adventure about a man named Henry. One day, he sailed out of the bay back his home in America. He was about to give up the next morning when he was spotted by a ship. He earned his passage by working as an unpaid hand. So he landed in London, penniless. When he was wondering on the pavement, Oliver and Rodrick were making a bet on him whether he could survive one month with a million pound bank note. When a letter was given to Henry, he felt confused and angry. With puzzle, he left the two brothers' home.

T: Good story. Fluent, natural and you have used many words learnt in class like "spot", "bet", "passage", etc.

【设计意图与教学效果】 作为词汇课的巩固环节,检测课堂效果是目的之一,更重要的是提供一个场景和机会让学生将一个课时的教学内容付诸实践。而选用复述的方式,可以最大化地保证所学词汇能够用于该复述情境下,同时由于阅读文章是学生熟知的,避免了学生无话可说,保证学生能够更好地关注目标词汇的使用。从本节课学生的产出看,学生词汇复现使用度高,词汇使用符合情境、符合用法,这证明充分利用阅读文本、重构词汇教学语境是词汇教学的有效途径。

四、教学反思

本课旨在研讨高中英语词汇课的有效教学方法。通过本课的实践,从教学效果看,充分利用阅读文本,重构词汇教学语境,明确词汇学习的分层目标和实施目标词汇的分层教学,运用思维导图搭建词汇学习网络是解决高中英语教师词汇教学诸多困惑的有效途径。

(一) 充分利用阅读文本,重构词汇教学语境

词汇教学与阅读教学相结合是高中英语词汇教学的重要途径。单元目标词汇往往集中在阅读文章中,而阅读文章本身就是一个理想的话题情境。合理地使用教材、深入挖掘文本能够为词汇课提供充足的语言素材和话题情境,能够减轻教师为寻找合适的话题带来的负担。另外,高中英语教材的阅读文本普遍偏长,生词偏多,发展学生高层次阅读理解技能的

任务逐渐加重，一个课时的阅读课，很难兼顾语言学习和深层理解。阅读文本的再次使用，能够加深学生理解该情境下需要掌握的词汇，更让繁重的学习任务化整为零，循序渐进地记忆学习，保持了学生持续的学习热情。因此，教师有必要再次梳理阅读文脉，重组阅读语篇，重构词汇语境，基于阅读语境呈现、操练和运用词汇，通过 Paraphrase、Retelling 和 Discussing 等活动进一步加深学生对阅读文本深层寓意的产出性理解。本节课的实践证明，基于阅读文本语境，以词汇学习和运用为主要目标的语篇层次的词汇教学尝试是有益的，有效的。学生的词汇学习有个接触、理解、记忆、运用、巩固的渐进过程，学习效果是有保障的。

（二）明确词汇学习的分层目标，实施目标词汇的分层教学

高中英语倡导学生通过语篇阅读理解词汇在语境中的意义。因此，不管一个单元的生词有多少个，多数生词会首次出现在阅读文本中。如果阅读课第一课时过度关注生词，就会影响阅读技能的培养。因此，教师应该对词汇进行分层教学。在阅读第一课时，教师应该更多关注生词在语境中的意义理解，关注那些用法和搭配对阅读理解有影响的生词，适当讲解以帮助学生在语用层面上解读文本，将词汇教学与阅读理解有机结合。总之，阅读课的词汇教学主要关注词汇的语境意义。作为侧重词汇教学的阅读课第二课时，教师备课的第一要务是整理筛选出重点词汇，明确哪些词汇需要掌握其音形义，哪些词汇是需要在语境中呈现、操练和运用，哪些词汇需要在新的语境中复用和活用。总之，教师需要明确词汇学习的分层目标，发展学生重点词汇的语用能力，词句单位的词汇教学更多关注词法和句法，语篇单位的词汇教学更多关注重点词汇在语境中的灵活运用。

（三）巧妙运用思维导图，搭建词汇学习网络

如何有效识记单词应该是一直以来困扰学生的一大难题，而思维导图作为一种显性的思维工具和学习方法，可以促进学生对词汇的理解和识记。教师往往会通过板书来呈现新词，然而传统的板书只能顾及词汇的拼写，往往会忽略单词的词性、意义和用法，而思维导图则可以让学生通过词语之间的联系去推测词性、意义和用法，使词汇内部的知识外显出来，学生对单词的理解也更具逻辑性。同时思维导图对词汇的识记也大有助益，学生可以通过思维导图来回顾所学词汇，使思维过程和记忆方法有迹可循，加深了记忆的痕迹，增强了记忆的效果。因此英语教师可以巧妙地运用思维导图，促进学生对词汇的理解，攻克单词"难记易忘"的难题。

总之，选用阅读情境、巧用思维导图，可以建立词汇之间的联系，可以发散词汇的学习内容，可以减轻教师词汇课备课负担，这样的教学是值得尝试的。

（课例撰写：温州第二中学　项纸陆　浙江师范大学　杨聪聪）

教材文本

THE MILLION POUND BANK NOTE

Act I, Scene 3

NARRATOR: It is the summer of 1903. Two old and wealthy brothers, Roderick and Oliver, have made a bet. Oliver believes that with a million pound bank note a man could survive a month in London. His brother Roderick doubts it. At this moment, they see a penniless young man **wandering** on the **pavement** outside their house. It is Henry Adams, an American **businessman**, who is lost in London and does not know what he should do.

RODERICK: Young man, would you step inside a moment, please?

HENRY: Who? Me, sir?

RODERICK: Yes, you.

OLIVER: Through the front door on your left.

HENRY: (A servant opens a door) Thanks.

SERVANT: Good morning, sir. Would you please come in? **Permit** me to lead the way, sir.

OLIVER: (Henry enters) Thank you, James. That will be all.

RODERICK: How do you do, Mr ... er ... ?

HENRY: Adams. Henry Adams.

OLIVER: Come and sit down, Mr. Adams.

HENRY: Thank you.

RODERICK: You're an American?

HENRY: That's right, from San Francisco.

RODERICK: How well do you know London?

HENRY: Not at all, it's my first trip here.

RODERICK: I wonder, Mr. Adams, if you'd mind us asking a few questions.

HENRY: Not at all. **Go** right **ahead**.

RODERICK: May we ask what you're doing in this country and what your plans are?

HENRY: Well, I can't say that I have any plans. I'm hoping to find work. As a matter of fact, I landed in Britain **by accident**.

OLIVER: How is that possible?

HENRY: Well, you see, back home I had my own boat. About a month ago, I was sailing out of the bay ... (his eyes **stare at** what is left of the brother's dinner on table)

OLIVER: Well, go on.

HENRY: Oh, yes. Well, towards nightfall I found myself carried out to sea by a strong wind. It was all my **fault**. I didn't know whether I could survive until morning. The next morning I'd just about *given myself up for lost* when I was spotted by a ship.

OLIVER: And it was the ship that brought you to England.

HENRY: Yes. The fact is that I earned my **passage** by working as an unpaid hand, which **accounts for** my appearance. I went to the American **embassy** to **seek** help, but ... (The brothers smile at each other.)

RODERICK: Well, you mustn't worry about that. It's an advantage.

HENRY: I'm afraid I don't quite follow you, sir.

RODERICK: Tell us, Mr. Adams, what sort of work did you do in America?

HENRY: I worked for a mining company. Could you offer me some kind of work here?

RODERICK: **Patience**, Mr. Adams. If you don't mind, may I ask you how much money you have?

HENRY: Well, to be honest, I have none.

OLIVER: (happily) What luck! Brother, what luck! (claps his hands together)

HENRY: Well, it may seem lucky to you but not to me! **On the contrary**, in fact. If this is your idea of some kind of joke, I don't think it's very funny. (Henry stands up to leave) Now if you'll excuse me, I think I'll be on my way.

RODERICK: Please don't go, Mr. Adams. You mustn't think we don't care about you. Oliver, give him the letter.

OLIVER: Yes, the letter. (gets it from a desk and gives it to Henry like a gift) The letter.

HENRY: (taking it carefully) For me?

RODERICK: For you. (Henry starts to open it) Oh, no, you mustn't open it. Not yet. You can't open it until two o'clock.

HENRY: Oh, this is silly.

RODERICK: Not silly. There's money in it. (calls to the servant) James?

HENRY：	Oh, no. I don't want your charity. I just want an honest job.
RODERICK：	We know you're hard-working. That's why we've given you the letter. James, show Mr. Adams out.
OLIVER：	Good luck, Mr. Adams.
HENRY：	Well, why don't you explain what this is all about?
RODERICK：	You'll soon know. (looks at the clock) In exactly an hour and a half.
SERVANT：	This way, sir.
RODERICK：	Mr. Adams, not until 2 o'clock. Promise?
HENRY：	Promise. Goodbye.

说课案例十（读写课）

PEP M5U4 Making the News

一、教学目标定位

各位老师大家好！刚刚我为大家呈现的是一节读写课。本课教材选自人教版高中英语教科书必修 5 第 4 单元 Making the News，单元的中心话题是"新闻"。阅读材料选自 Reading 部分，题目为"Unforgettable", says new journalist。文章的主要内容是新手记者 Zhou Yang 和上司 Hu Xin 之间的对话，谈话内容涉及新闻工作者需要具备的素质、技能和采访的基本流程以及一些注意事项。

首先，让我们一起简要分析一下教材。文章的标题往往能够起到提纲挈领的作用，而本课标题中 unforgettable 一词充分说明了 Hu Xin 的话对 Zhou Yang 的职业生涯产生的重要作用。文章正文前两行背景介绍的文字交代了对话双方的关系，其中 Never will Zhou Yang forget ... 和 strongly influence 等表达的使用不仅点了题，也充分说明 how to be a good journalist 这部分内容是文章的重点。这两行文字概括了文章的大意，有助于学生迅速把握文本主旨。正文由对话形式呈现，可以分为三部分，分别从 how to work in a team、how to cover an accurate story 以及 how to avoid accusation 三方面介绍了一名优秀记者所需的素质和技能。文章中虽然有大量的口头表达，通俗易懂，但由于学生对这类体裁的文本可能比较陌生，而且文章内容涉及新闻领域的专业知识，有不少习惯表达和专业术语，如 get the wrong end of the stick 等，是阅读的一个难点。文章大意的理解并不难，在知道词汇字面意思的基础上，绝大部分细节的理解还是容易的。

因此，基于对文章特点的把握，我开设了一节读写课，读文章脉络，构建写作框架；读文本信息，输入写作内容；读语言知识，运用词汇表达。为此，我设置了如下的语言知识和技能目标。首先，学生能够通过扫读和跳读获取文章中关于成为一名优秀记者所需要的素质和技能的内容，并将其用于写作中。其次，学生能够根据文章细节划分段落和概括大意，并根据三段大意构建写作框架。最后，学生能够根据阅读任务，利用上下文猜词或忽略非关键性词汇表达等方法，充分理解 unforgettable 和 cover 等词在文章中的意思，并在写作中使用 cover、submit、professional photographer 等与新闻报道直接或间接相关的表达。本节课的教学重点是概括文章三部分的大意并将其作为写作框架，用自己的语言完成 summary 的写作。而本节课的教学难点是采用适当的策略，或利用上下文猜词或忽略非关键性词汇，理解新词和行业习语，并用自己的话传达出文章的大意。

以上是我对教材的简要分析和教学目标的定位，接下来是教学目标的达成情况。

二、教学目标达成

从本节课的教学效果看，读写整合的综合技能课使得课堂教学节奏紧凑，教学步骤环环相扣，教学内容聚焦，教学目标达成度高。首先，学生通过阅读文章标题和介绍性文字，根据 unforgettable、never will forget、strongly influence 等关键表达知晓了人物的职业和关系，并对下文的内容作出了推测，为后面正文的阅读做好了充分的准备。接下来，在教师提出阅读的核心任务后，学生开始阅读和找寻文章中关于如何成为优秀记者的内容。在教师的引导下，学生将文章分为三个片段，依次找出了各个部分中的相关信息，并根据细节概括出了大意。同时，我还引导学生通过关注 mean 等信号词和利用上下文猜词的方法来自主理解 have a good nose 等核心表达，学生能很好地运用这些策略达成语言知识目标。在获取文本内容的同时，我还将三部分的大意和关键词呈现在黑板上，有意识地引导学生发现提取文章的框架和关键信息，可为之后的写作做铺垫。三段大意可以作为写作中三部分的主题句，循序渐进地构建写作框架，同时帮助学生意识到关键词也可以用于写作中。这些步骤是学生前期对文章的框架、内容以及语言的输入过程。在课堂后阶段，学生根据这些已有的输入，运用自己的语言如 linking words 的使用，完成了 summary 的写作，然后从写作框架、内容和语言三方面对同伴的习作进行了简要的评价。这是后期的输出过程，是这节课的生成。除了个别的语法错误，抽选出来的学生习作基本上能做到框架清晰、关键信息齐全和语言表达准确等，说明学生先前的输入和铺垫做得比较到位，学生的输出效果比较理想。此外，本节课的教学还实现了布鲁姆的认知目标分类理论中理解、分析、运用、创造和评价等目标。学生在理解文本的基础上，通过分析和提取关键信息构建了写作框架，并运用文中的新词和自己的语言进行了习作的创作，最后通过同伴之间的互相评价巩固了所学和所用。

接下来是我对这节课教学的反思。

三、教学效果反思

本节课是我对于阅读读后活动的思考，也是利用读写整合的形式解决读后活动中存在的种种问题的尝试。读后活动本应该成为阅读课的高潮,却又往往因为其在内容、形式、时间以及学生的主观认知上的限制,成为阅读课的败笔。通过这节课的实践,我认识到读写整合是一种非常行之有效的方法,是阅读和写作的完美结合,也是读中和读后的完美结合。对于这节读写课,我有以下两点反思。

第一点,读写整合,使读中任务重点突出,难点容易突破

阅读的目的不仅仅是纯粹的语言学习或信息内容的获取,它是一个综合的过程。在这个过程中,无论是语言的学习,还是内容的获取都应该为写作的输出做铺垫。因此,与这一目的无关的其他教学内容都无需过多关注,这样教学的重点自然就会突出,学生更容易抓住重心,课堂教学的节奏就能更加紧凑,收放自如。与此同时,由于学习目标明确,我更容易分析出学生在获取相应的内容与语言时可能遇到的困难,从而做好充分的准备,通过各种方式为学生搭建脚手架,帮助学生完成学习任务。因此,在读写课中教师是一个引导者,学生的学习方式、学习过程和学习评价是课堂的核心和关注的焦点。比如这节课中,我在课前通过细致充分的文本解读,提取出文章的脉络作为写作框架;在课堂中引导学生阅读不同部分,忽略一些不影响阅读信息获取的语言,指导学生在上下文中猜测关键词,这样一来,学生在学习过程中就能重点把握文章中关于 how to be a good journalist 的语言和内容,这样阅读过程就节奏紧凑,过程也更加流畅,效率也更高。

第二点,读写整合,让读后写作结构清晰,内容语言丰富

在设计读后活动时,我常常苦于寻找合适的活动形式和话题。小组讨论、访谈和辩论等形式实行力不高,而与阅读文本同一话题或不同话题则较难把握方向。我也常常苦于选择合适的语言,运用本节课语言,当堂课输出难以落实;使用学生已学的语言,词汇目标则落实不到位。而本课读写整合教学的尝试成功实现了在话题保持一致的前提下,学生基于阅读文本的内容,使用阅读中抽取的语篇框架和学习的新词汇,并用自己的语言表述同样的内容。学生与文本之间存在着一定的信息差,保证教师在设计写作任务时能够根据班级学生的能力设置难度适宜的写作任务,并为学生设置一定的教学梯度,满足不同学生在不同阶段的学习需求。正因为读后的写作任务与阅读紧密结合,因此阅读任务变得更有意义,同时写作任务也变得更加轻松。两者相得益彰,相辅相成。

当然,本节课也存在着一些不足。比如,留给学生阅读和思考的时间不够,学生在进行写作输出时时间比较紧张,整节课的教学节奏有点快。

以上是我对这节课教材的分析、目标的设定和达成情况以及教学的反思,请大家多多指教,谢谢大家!

(说课稿撰写:温州第二中学 项纸陆 浙江师范大学 朱梦佳)

附：教学课例及教材文本

M5U4 Making The News

一、课例背景

走进英语阅读课课堂，常常惊叹于教师读前环节设计的精心，或解决词汇障碍，或输入背景知识，或引发思考，或活跃气氛；常常沉浸于读中环节设计的精妙，或深入浅出，或层层铺垫，或环环相扣，或发人深省。但是，在读后环节，常常看到读后任务与阅读输入主题联系不紧密，甚至偏离主题及教学重点；或读后产出形式单一，内容空洞，产出质量较差，展现不出学生从文本中获取信息内容、学到的语言知识等；或读后活动因时间分配不均，匆匆结束；或读后活动形式内容幼稚，不符合学生的认知特点和知识水平。那么，如何让读后活动精彩起来、丰富起来、实用起来，就成为高中英语教师关注的焦点之一，而读写整合正是解决这一问题的有效教学策略之一。因为，写的性质是产出，保证读中输入的信息内容和语言知识有效地体现；写的形式多种多样，任务的难度有高有低，保证输出满足学生各阶段不同的认知需求；写的任务要求课堂时间分配合理，但这样能够保证阅读内容的筛选，保证课堂重点突出；更为重要的是，写能够成为一节课的目标，以写为目标驱动，设计阅读活动，保证阅读能够实在、实用、实效。

二、教学分析

（一）教材分析

本课教材选自人教版《普通高中课程标准实验教科书英语必修5》第四单元。本单元的中心话题是"新闻"，内容涉及新闻工作者应该具备的素质、技能、注意事项和新闻采访的基本程序等。本阅读材料选自 Reading 部分，通过 Zhou Yang，一个跃跃欲试的新手记者和上司 Hu Xin 之间的谈话，向学生展示了新闻工作者应该具备的素质、技能以及采访的基本流程和一些注意事项。文章在展现两人对话之前有一标题和两行介绍性的话语。

标题往往能够起到提纲挈领的作用，正如该标题中 unforgettable 一词正是起到了该作用，充分说明了 Hu Xin 的话对 Zhou Yang 的职业生涯产生的巨大作用，对他今后工作起到了重要的借鉴作用。而应用文体中说明性的语言往往带有背景的交代以及对下文的概述，而该文中，前两行的文字交代了对话中的人物以及他们的身份特征，其中 Never will Zhou Yang forget ...；strongly influence 等词句的使用不仅点题，表明了 how to be a good journalist 这部分内容是文章的重点。该部分内容能够很好地提示学生文章的中心大意，对快速获得文章内容信息有着极为重要的作用。正文可分为三部分，分别从如何在团队中协作、如何报道准确的新闻、如何免受控告三方面讲述了成为优秀记者的素质、技能和建议。

文章虽然以对话的形式呈现,文中有大量的口头表达,通俗易懂,但是由于文章涉及专业领域的知识,有不少习惯用语,如 get the wrong end of the stick 等,以及与新闻行业有关的知识内容,或成为阅读的一个难点。

(二) 学生分析

本班学生通过前三个学期的学习,能够基本独立完成篇章阅读,能够利用上下文理解生词,能够使用适当的阅读技能和策略获得相应的信息内容,完成难度不高的阅读任务。但是仍处于语言学习初级阶段的他们,还不能自主分析难词、推断信息,还不能自主概括段落大意、抽取文章框架,还不能自主构建写作框架,完成任务写作。因此完成本节课的读写活动,他们会有一定的困难。本班学生性格内向,喜欢独立完成任务,因此课堂上活动多设计个体活动。同样,因为该阶段的学生不喜欢情景对话、虚构的角色表演,因此读后任务写作是一项能够很好满足学生认知需求的活动。

(三) 教学目标

1. 语言能力与学习能力

1) 能够根据标题和介绍性语段中的关键词预测全文;

2) 能够根据阅读任务,利用上下文猜词或忽略非关键性词汇等方法理解 unforgettable、cover 等在文中的意思,从而理解文章,并在习作中使用 cover、submit、professional photographer 等与新闻报道直接或间接相关的语言;

3) 能够根据段落中的细节概括大意,利用阅读获得的写作框架、写作内容、写作语言进行独立写作,并对写作框架、写作内容和写作语言进行简单评价。

2. 文化意识与思维品质

能够知道关于新闻报告的基本流程步骤,以及成为优秀记者需要的素质、技能和经验;能够体会到从事新闻报告的记者的苦与乐。

(四) 教学重点

1. 能够概括文章三部分的中心大意,并将其作为写作框架进行任务写作;

2. 能够抽取关于如何成为优秀记者的素质、技能以及建议的相关信息,转述对话内容,并对部分内容进行调整,使用文章中出现的部分新词,并用自己的语言完成写作任务。

(五) 教学难点

1. 能够准确概括文章三部分的中心大意;

2. 能够采取适当策略或利用上下文或忽略非关键性词汇,理解新词和行业习语;

3. 能够通过自己的语言,转述文章内容,并对文章内容作出相应的调整。

（六）教学思路

本课围绕着如何成为优秀的记者展开，通过阅读获取信息内容和写作框架，其次为写作提供必要的语言支持；通过写作检测学生阅读获取信息的能力，提供语言使用的载体，输出新获得的知识与信息。首先，通过阅读文章标题和介绍性文字，了解对话双方的基本信息，根据 unforgettable、never will … forget 和 strongly influence 等语言，推测文章内容，知道是上司对刚来的下属传送经验，讲述如何成为优秀的记者。接着，通过教师引导，分三部分阅读文章，要求学生先找出每部分关于如何成为优秀记者的信息，然后根据细节概括大意。最后根据获得的写作框架和内容，用自己的语言完成习作。

三、教学实录

步骤一：读前预测，获背景、大意

Read the title and the first two lines ahead of the conversation. Pay attention to the key words and predict the content of the talk.

T： Today, we are going to read something we are not quite familiar with. It's about news report. Now, open your books and turn to page 26. Look through the passage, and tell me whether it is the same with those readings we have read.

S1： No, it is different.

T： What is different?

S1： It is a … two people …

T： (Nodding) Two people's talk. It is a conversation. Right?

S1： Yeah.

T： Good, sit down please. And ahead of the talk, you can find two lines, right?

Ss： Yes.

T： Usually it is an introduction about the talk, or some background information. It can be important because we can get much information from this part. Now, let's read the title and the first two lines. Pay attention to some words you think are informative.

Ss： (Read)

T： Who are the talkers?

Ss： Zhou Yang and Hu Xin.

T： What are they?

S2： Zhou Yang is a journalist.

T： What kind of journalist? Experienced?

S2： No, he is a new journalist.

T： Yes, a NEW (stressed) journalist. What about Hu Xin?

S3： He is Zhou Yang's boss.

- T： What can you infer from the words "unforgettable, never will Zhou Yang forget and strongly influence"? Remember Zhou Yang is a green hand and Hu Xin is his boss.
- S4： Hu Xin is going to say something important to Zhou Yang.
- T： What is important to Zhou Yang?
- S4： Maybe some experience or …
- T： What do you think?
- S5： Hu Xin is going to tell Zhou Yang what to do.
- T： To do what?
- S5： How to be a good journalist.
- T： So you think this talk is about how to become a good journalist, right?
- S5： Yes.
- T： I agree. Thank you, take your seat please. In order to tell Zhou Yang how to become a good, or successful journalist (note on blackboard), what exactly will Hu Xin mention?
- S6： Skills.
- S7： Experiences.
- S8： Qualities.
- S9： Advice.
- T： Good job, everyone. So we are going to read this passage, and our central reading task is to read for qualities, skills and advice to become a successful journalist.

【效果与反思】 该部分的阅读任务跟传统意义上的读前活动有所不同。传统意义上,读前活动往往是选用与文章相关话题进行口笔头的交际训练,或扫清词汇障碍或解决背景知识,然后阅读标题,预测文本内容。本节课中,读前活动指正文前的阅读,包括标题和介绍性语句。该活动的进行,充分利用了标题概括文章中心思想的作用,利用了介绍性语段输入的对话背景,理清人物关系,并利用关键词,推测了文章的大致内容,提出了阅读的核心任务,对接下来的阅读框架和内容的获得起到了铺垫的作用。

步骤二：读中理解,获内容、框架

A：片段一阅读

Read from line 3 to line 15. This is the first section, mainly focusing on how to work in a team. Students are going to read this part together, pick out information about how to become a successful journalist and then summarize the main idea of this section.

- T： Now, everyone, read from line 13 to line 15. While reading, underline the words and sentences about how to become a successful journalist. Here we go.
- Ss： (Read the corresponding lines)

T: What have you got?

S10: First we'll put you as an assistant to an experienced journalist.

T: Yeah, first, an assistant to an experienced journalist. (Note on blackboard) You?

S11: Later you can cover a story and submit the article yourself.

T: Right, cover and submit a story. (Note on blackboard) Anything else?

S12: You'll find your colleagues very eager to assist you.

T: Especially who?

S12: ... (Puzzled)

T: Can you help him?

S13: A professional photographer.

T: Yes, a professional photographer. (Note on blackboard) Now, everyone, based on all the details, what is this part mainly about?

Ss: (Think)

T: S14, you can have a try.

S14: About ... Er ...

T: Thank you anyway. Everyone, will Zhou Yang work alone? Or?

Ss: In a team.

T: So this section is about how to work ...

Ss: In a team.

T: (Note on blackboard)

【效果与反思】 之所以将文章分为三部分进行阅读，除了学生全文阅读并找寻信息有难度外，还因为教师将文章作者的写作脉络以阅读任务的方式呈现给学生，要求学生根据不同的细节概括出每一部分的大意，可以使学生明白文章是从三个方面讲述了如何成为一名成功的记者。如此，阅读的任务分散到各个部分，使得学生的注意力更容易集中，任务完成质量更高，学生完成任务的成就感更强；在完成正文阅读的同时，学生不仅获得了关于如何成为一名成功记者的内容，也获得了写作框架，一举两得。针对于该部分，教师关注内容的获取，对于文章中出现的 admirable，unusual 等词并不多加关注，因为该类词汇并不影响学生的阅读理解和信息获得，教师可将该类词汇留作下节课的知识点。因此，本课的重点突出，难点容易突破，学生只关注信息的获得，并能够将其作为写作内容呈现在习作之中。

B. 片段二阅读

Read from line 16 to line 29. This is the second section, mainly focusing on how to cover an accurate story. Students are going to read this part, pick out information about how to become a successful journalist and then summarize the main idea of this section.

T: Now, let's read to line 29. Boys, you are going to read Hu Xin's lines and girls, you are going to read Zhou Yang's lines. While reading, still remember to underline the information about how to become a successful journalist. Now, girls, ready? Go!

Ss: (Read this section)

T: What have you got?

S15: Ask many different questions.

T: Yes. (Note on blackboard) Continue.

S15: Don't miss your deadline, don't be rude, don't talk too much.

T: Three "Don'ts". (Note on blackboard) These are Hu Xin's ...

S15: Advice.

T: Right. Anything else?

S15: (Shake her head)

T: Ok, sit down. S16, have you found more?

S16: Yes, listening carefully.

T: Yes. While listening, what else should be done?

S16: Take notes.

T: Right. Sit down, please. Listen and take notes. (Note on blackboard) This is one more skill. How about S17?

S17: Have a good nose.

T: That's right. How do you understand this expression?

S17: Know what is going on.

T: Right, but we can find there is a word indicating the meaning of this expression. Which one?

Ss: That means.

T: Right. So what is the meaning of the expression?

S18: Be able to assess when people are not telling the truth.

T: So if the interviewee is not telling the truth, what should a journalist do?

S19: Do some researches.

T: Good, that's right. (Note on blackboard) Now, according to all the details, what is the main idea of this section?

Ss: (Think)

T: What is you answer?

S20: This section is about how to cover a story.

T: What kind of story?

S20: En ... Good story.

T: Not bad. It is about how to cover an accurate story.

【效果与反思】 在任务的驱动下,学生完成该部分的积极性较高,通过前面步骤的铺垫,学生完成信息寻找的任务并不困难。虽然该部分生词较少,但是关于成为优秀记者的技能涉及较多,因此,学生很难一次性将答案呈现出来,所以教师通过引导不同学生,集众人之力,将文中信息呈现在黑板上(板书包括三个部分所提炼出来的关于成为成功记者的重点,除了呈现文本的脉络和信息,也能在学生习作过程中起到提示的作用)。本段中,学生在理解 have a good nose 和 assess 等核心词汇时有一定的困难,因此教师通过引导学生关注信号词、上下文等方式引导学生自主理解生词。

C：片段三阅读

Read from line 30 to line 41. This is the third section, mainly focusing on how to protect a story from accusations. Students are going to read this part silently by themselves, pick out relevant information and then summarize the main idea of this section.

T： Now read the last section. Think about what is the story about? Why does Hu Xin mention the story?

Ss：(Read)

T： S21, what is this story about?

S21： It is about a footballer taking money and not scoring goals deliberately.

T： Yes, and the journalist reported it?

S21： Yes.

T： Was he sure about the details?

S21： No.

T： We know the result of the report. The report was proved right. Then, what if it is not?

S21： The footballer could have demanded damages.

T： It means if the report was not right, the journalist would be accused. Then, why does Hu Xin tell Zhou Yang this story?

S22： To tell him how to avoid accusations. Some suggestions.

T： Good, yes. How to protect a story from accusations. (Note on blackboard) Then, how?

S23： He needs evidence.

T： How can a journalist collect evidence? You can read the lines just ahead.

S24： Do researches and use a recorder.

T： Good. (Note on blackboard)

【效果与反思】 最后一部分讲述的故事与第二部分有着密切的关系,学生直接概括大意是有困难的。因此,教师通过引导学生关注该部分之前的语句,让学生将控告和证据联系在一起,让获取证据与做调查联系在一起,如此,概括大意就显得顺理成章。从整体上来看,教师的阅读任务的设置主要是为了获得需要的信息内容,在不影响学生理解的情况下,对于语言的处理"浅尝辄止",教学重点得以突出,教学难点得以突破。通过阅读,学生在知识上、内容上、心理上都做好了充分准备,写作的导入、操作水到渠成。

步骤三：读后习作,产知识、技能

T: Now, we have got all the information about how to become a good journalist. It is time for you to write. You need to pick out the information from the talk. Reorganize the points. Put them under three sections. What are the three sections?

Ss: How to work in a team, how to cover an accurate story, how to protect a story from accusations.

T: Right. While you are organizing your ideas, you need to use some proper linking words so that your writing can be logical. Let's do the first part as an example. He has to learn how to work in a team. First ...

Ss: He should be an assistant to an experienced journalist.

T: Until he is experienced, he ...

Ss: He can cover and submit a story by himself.

T: While he is walking, he will be assisted by ...

Ss: By a professional photographer to take photographs.

T: Good, now, you have understood how to write. I have given you the beginning as well as the three points, and you are going to finish this writing about how to become a successful journalist.

Ss: (Write)

T: You have finished writing. Let's read one of our classmates' and comment on it.

Ss: (Read)

T: What about the content? Does he include most of the points about how to become a successful journalist?

Ss: Yes.

T: So, content, good. What about the structure? Clear?

Ss: Yes.

T: Why?

S25: He used proper linking words.

T: What about the language?

S26: I think good. Just a few mistakes. The sentences are long and a lot of new words are used.

T: Now, let's read another one's and comment on it.

Ss: (Read)

T: S27, what are your comments on it?

S27: It is good. He included all the points about how to become a good journalist. He used some linking words so it is clear to read. The language is good for there is no mistake and he used most of the bold-faced words. So, it is good.

T: And he is good because, besides all you have mentioned, he reorganized some of the points on the blackboard. And he used his own words to express all the points. Of course, this is a good writing.

【效果与反思】 写作之前教师先说明写作任务,并提供开头,引导学生关注框架,示范如何使用连接词。在阅读所获得的内容的基础上,绝大部分学生能够顺利写作,并呈现了质量相对较高的作文。作为本课的读后活动,写作任务的话题与阅读话题保持一致,内容来自阅读,框架提取于阅读,新的语言学得于阅读,因此,本课真正做到了读写相辅相成,读写有机结合。作为本课生成的教学目标,最后的写作评价,通过教师的引导示范,优秀学生的示范点评,学生能够领会优秀习作应从写作构思、写作内容和写作语言上努力,为学生整个的学习起到了承上启下的作用。

四、教学反思

本课是笔者对于阅读读后活动的思考,是通过读写整合的方式解决读后活动的存在的种种问题的尝试。读后活动由于其在内容、形式、时间分配、学生的主观认知上的限制,本应成为阅读课的高潮,却又往往成为阅读课的败笔。因此,通过本课的实践,笔者认为读写整合是一种行之有效的方式,是阅读与写作的完美结合,是读中和读后的完美结合。

(一) 读写整合,让读中任务重点突出,难点容易突破

阅读的目的不单单是纯粹语言学习,也不单单是信息内容获取,它是一个综合的过程。在这个过程中,不论是内容的获取,还是语言的学习都是为了写作的输出做铺垫。因此与这一目的无关的教学内容都不作为本节课的知识,教学的重点自然就会突出,学生容易抓住重心,课堂教学节奏紧凑,收放自如。与此同时,因为学习目标明确,教师容易分析出学生在获得相应的语言与内容时可能遇到的困难,就能够做好充分准备,通过各种方式为学生搭建脚手架,帮助学生完成学习任务。因此,读写课上,教师的角色只是一位指导者或引导者,学生的学习方式、学习过程、学习评价是课堂的核心、关注的焦点。比如本课中,教师课前通过细致的文本解读,抽取文章的框架(即写作框架),课中引导学生阅读不同部分,引导学生忽略部分不影响阅读信息获取的语言,指导学生通过上下文猜测等方式解决关键性词汇的理解,因此学生重点关注如何成为一名优秀的记者的内容与语言,教学过程流畅、节奏紧凑,学生阅读理解率高。

(二) 读写整合,让读后写作结构清晰,内容语言丰富

每当设计读后活动,我常常苦于寻找形式:对话,学生不积极;访谈,学生不乐意;辩论,学生没能力。我常常苦于寻找话题:同一话题,口头表述没有信息差;不同话题,容易出现内容偏题。我常常苦于寻找语言:使用本课语言,很难落实;使用学生已学语言,偏离本课目标。

因此，通过本课的读写整合案例，印证了在话题保持一致的前提下，学生能够利用阅读文本的内容，使用阅读中抽取的框架，活用阅读中学习的新词汇表述同样的内容；学生与文本作者之间存在一定的信息差，保证教师能够根据班级学生的能力设置难度适当的写作任务，并为学生设置教学梯度，能够满足不同学生在不同阶段的学习需求。正因为读后的写作任务与阅读关系密切，使得阅读任务变得更有意义，同时也使得写作任务变得轻松。两者相得益彰，相辅相成。

(课例撰写：温州第二中学　项纸陆　浙江师范大学　朱梦佳)

教材文本

My first work assignment
"Unforgettable", says new journalist

Never will I Zhou Yang (ZY) forget his first assignment at the office of a popular English newspaper. His discussion with his new boss, Hu Xin (HX), was to strongly influence his life as a journalist.

HX: Welcome. We're delighted you're coming to work with us. Your first job here will be an assistant journalist. Dou you have any questions?

ZY: Can I go out on a story immediately?

HX: (laughing) That's admirable, but I'm afraid it would be unusual! Wait till you're more experienced. First we'll put you as an assistant to an experience journalist. Later you can cover a story and submit the article yourself.

ZY: Wonderful! What do I need to take with me? I already have a notebook and camera.

HX: No need for a camera. You'll have a professional photography with you to take photographs. You'll find your colleagues very eager to assist you, so you may be able to concentrate on photography later if you're interested.

ZY: Thank you. Not only am I interested in photography, but I took an amateur course at university to update my skills.

HX: Good.

ZY: What do I need to remember when I go out to cover a story?

HX: You need to be curious. Only if you ask as many different questions will you acquire all the information you need to know. We say a good journalist must have a good "nose" for a story. That means you must be able to assess when people are not telling the whole truth and then try to discover it. They must use research to inform themselves of the missing parts of the story.

ZY: What should I keep in mind?

HX: Here comes my list of dos and don'ts: don't miss your deadline, don't be rude, don't talk too much, but make sure you listen to the interviewee carefully.

ZY: Why is listening so important?

HX: Well, you have to listen for detailed facts. Meanwhile you have to prepare the next question depending on what the person says.

ZY: But how can I listen carefully while taking notes?

HX: That is a trick of the trade. If the interviewee agrees, you can use a recorder to get the facts straight. It's also useful if a person wants to challenge you. You have the evidence to support your story.

ZY: I see! Have you ever had a case where someone accused your journalist of getting the wrong end of the stick?

HX: Yes, but it was a long time ago. This is how the story goes. A footballer was accused of taking money or deliberately not scoring goals so as to let the other team win. We went to interview him. He denied taking money but we were skeptical. So we arranged an interview between the footballer and the man supposed to bribe him. When we saw them together we guessed from the footballer's body language that he was not telling the truth. So we wrote an article suggesting he was guilty. It was a dilemma because the footballer could have demanded damages if we were wrong. He tried to stop us publishing it but later we were proved right.

ZY: Wow! That was a real "scoop". I'm looking forward to my first assignment now. Perhaps I'll get a scoop too!

HX: Perhaps you will. You never know.

主要参考文献

1. 方贤忠.如何说课[M].上海:华东师范大学出版社,2008.
2. 罗晓杰.多媒体辅助英语"说课"研究[J].外语电化教学,2003(12).
3. 罗晓杰.说课及其策略[J].教育科学研究,2005(02).
4. 罗晓杰.试论英语说课讲稿的撰写[J].课程·教材·教法,2002(04).
5. 罗晓杰,牟金江,项纸陆.中学英语读写课教学设计与说课[M].长春:吉林文化音像出版社,2010.
6. 罗晓杰,牟金江.如何说英语课——方法与艺术[M].上海:华东师范大学出版社,2012.
7. 罗晓杰,叶志雄.说课及其评价指标体系研究[J].黑龙江高教研究,2004(06).
8. 牟金江,罗晓杰,项纸陆.英语学科知识与教学能力·高中版[M].上海:华东师范大学出版社,2013.
9. 牟金江,罗晓杰,项纸陆.高中英语"三段七步"读写整合教学法[M].福州:福建教育出版社,2015.
10. 周玲,罗晓杰,项纸陆.英语教师说课技能存在的问题与对策[J].基础教育外语教学研究,2011(03).